William Maccrillis Griswold

A Descriptiv List of Novels and Tales Dealing with History of North America

William Maccrillis Griswold

A Descriptiv List of Novels and Tales Dealing with History of North America

ISBN/EAN: 9783337047306

Printed in Europe, USA, Canada, Australia, Japan

Cover: Foto ©ninafisch / pixelio.de

More available books at **www.hansebooks.com**

A DESCRIPTIV LIST

OF

NOVELS AND TALES

DEALING WITH THE

HISTORY OF NORTH AMERICA.

COMPILED BY
W. M. GRISWOLD.

CAMBRIDGE, MASS:
W. M. GRISWOLD, PUBLISHER.
1895.

Descriptive Lists of Historical Novels, Part I., Ancient Life, Price $.50.

HISTORY FOR READY REFERENCE, from the best historians, biographers, and specialists; [by J. N. Larned: In 5 vols.: Springfield, Mass., *C. A. Nichols Co.*, 1894.] The compiler says that—"The entire contents of this work . . . hav been carefully culled from some thousands of books—embracing the whole range (in English) of standard historical writing, both general and special; the biography, the institutional and constitutional studies, the social investigations, the archeological researches, the ecclesiastical and religious discussions, and all other important tributaries to the great and swelling stream of historical knoledge. It has been culled as one might pic choice fruits, careful to choose the perfect and the ripe, where such ar found, and careful to keep their flavor unimpaired . . . History as written by those, on one hand, who hav depicted its scenes most vividly, and on the other, by those who hav searched its facts, weighed its evidences, and pondered its meanings most critically and deeply, is given in their words . . . The whole matter is presented under an arrangement which imparts distinctness to its topics, while shoing them in their sequence and in all their large relations, both national and international." The scheme is excellent, and the editorial work has been done admirably. The maps, also, ar of great value. But the extremely small type in which the work is printed, and the size and weight of the volumes, will limit its use to such persons as can consult it in the reference department of public libraries. Had the work been published in volumes half as large and four times as numerous it could cordially be recommended as forming a family library of history. It would hav been found especially useful where the family included school-children; but in vue of the carelessness of young persons in reading, if it suits their convenience, by a bad light, and inattention to the withdrawal of sun-light at the close of the day, its use, even as a dictionary, should be watched carefully.

Index to St. Nicholas, Vols. I.-XXI., Price $1.

28485

AMERICAN HISTORICAL NOVELS.

BEHEMOTH, a Legend of the Mound Builders [by Cornelius Mathews (1815-89): N. Y., Langley, 1838.] "Is a short romance, conducted with skill as to the mere mechanism of the story, and colored by an imagination which has studied external nature in her most beautiful aspects. 'It was the main design of the author,' he says, 'to make the gigantic relics which ar found scattered throughout this continent, subservient to the purposes of the imagination. He has, therefore, dared to evoke a mity creature from the earth, and striven to clothe him with life and motion. Coeval with this, the great race which preceded the red men as the possessors of our continent hav been called into being.' Hence we hav Behemoth in his huge terrors, threatening the cities of the Mound-builders,—with their attempts by force and cunning to destroy the monstrous mischief." [Illuminated Mag.]—"This work embodies a fine conception—a grand subject for the imagination. We ar carried into remote antiquity, when the great valley of the west was filled with a people whose power and skill ar attested in the relics of those vast and strange structures which hav survived the lapse of thousands of years. Long before the point of time, however, at which the story opens, the mastodon, whose enormous bones ar stil extant, had been exterminated—all except one—and his existence had, for many years, been a dim tradition among the mound-builders. He now appears—the survivor and avenger of his race—moving in the darkness of a single night, over the 5000 cities of the land, crushing forests, people, dwellings, towers, and sacred mounds—everything, beneath his feet." [N. Y. Review. 530

As collateral reading may be mentioned:—

CHILDREN'S STORIES IN AMERICAN HISTORY. [by Henrietta Christina Wright: Scribner, 1885.] "The story of Pocahontas is told as if its mythical character had not been fully exposed. Worse than this is the account of the Mound-builders, in chapter ii., making them out to hav been the Hyksos, after their expulsion from Egypt!" [Nation. 535

1492.

MERCEDES OF CASTILE [by Ja. Fenimore Cooper: Phil'a, 1840] describes Columbus' voyage. 540

1520.

CALAVAR; or The Knight of the Conquest [by Ro. Montgomery Bird (1803-54): Phil'a, Carey, 1834] "is certainly the best American novel, excepting perhaps one or two of Cooper's, which we hav read. If boldness of design, vigor of thôt, copiousness and power of language, thrilling incident, and graphic and magnificent description, can constitute a good novel, this is one. For the first 50 or 60 pages it is confessedly somewhat heavy; still the reader will perceive that a master-spirit is at work, to whose guidance he confidingly trusts. In a short time the whole interest of the narrativ rushes upon him; he gazes in imagination upon the Eden-like valleys of Mexico; he throbs with pain at the spectacle of slautered thousands of brave aborigines, and he sympathizes with the tender sorrees and heroic sufferings of the only female who figures in the story, and she too in the unwomanly garb of a page... Jacinto, alias Leila, is nevertheless a most delightful vision,—seen always under unfavorable circumstances, —but when seen, winding around the heart of the reader in spite of himself, —a beautiful, modest, heroic boy,—and yet a girl,—the discovery of whose sex, tho anticipated, does not beam upon the reader until toards the end... The description of the flight of the Spaniards over the dike of Lacuba, and of the horrors of the 'Melancholy night,' so called in history, is awfully sublime. In truth the whole work abounds in powerful delineation both of character and scenery, and it is with pride that we hail it as at once assuming and commanding a proud rank in the department of historical romance." [Southern Lit. Messenger].—" The author has studied with great care the costumes, manners, and military usages of the nativs, and has done for them what Cooper has done for the wild tribes of the north,—touched their rude features with the bright coloring of a poetic fancy. He has been equally fortunate in his delineations of the picturesque scenery of the land; and if he has been

less so in attempting to revive the antique dialog of the Spanish cavalier, we must not be surprised: nothing is more difficult than the skilful execution of a modern antique." [W: H. Prescott.] —" With the exception of Prescott's magnificent annals, we ar not acquainted with any work from which so clear a conception of those times can be gathered as from Calavar. It is crowded with graphic descriptions and scenes of intense excitement. The author revels among the variegated vegetation of that sunny clime, and sings the beauty of the blac-eyed fair ones with a rhapsodist's enthusiasm." [Quoted in Allibone. 545

INFIDEL, The, or the Fall of Mexico. [by R. M. Bird: Phil'a, Carey, 1835.] "The period at which the narrativ begins is a few months after the disastrous retreat of the Spaniards, during the 'Noche Triste,' so wonderfully described in Calavar. Cortez had reorganized his forces, reunited his allies, and was preparing for the siege of Mexico, now rendered strong in its defences by the valor, enterprise and activity of the new emperor, Guatimozin. The hero of the story, Juan Lerma, a former protegé of Cortez, but who had fallen under his displeasure, is the pivot on which the main interest of the work is made to turn. He is imprisoned, and ultimately rescued by Guatimozin, who carries him to Mexico. The details of a treasonable plot against the Captain General, headed by Villafana, one of the most complicated of villains, is skilfully interwoven with this portion of the narrativ." [Southern Lit. Messenger. 550

MONTEZUMA, by E: Maturin (1812-81): N. Y., Paine, 1845. 555

MALMITZIC THE TOLTEC, AND THE CAVALIERS OF THE CROSS. [by

W: Whiteman Fosdick (1825-62): Cin'ti, More, 1851.] "From the first line to the end the author assumes and sustains so lofty and grandiloquent a style that criticism, startled and appalled, lets fall her bowie, and first attempts a demonstration by marshalling to her aid Milton, Ossian, and Croly, but finding that neither comes up to the mark, brings in Pollock as a 'corps de reserve,' and, foiled again, admits that the whole 'course of time' cannot furnish a parallel, drops her balances in disgust, and quits the field ... Malmitzic is a terrible fello; and soon after the book opens—being inclined that way—gets into the thickest of a quarrel about a certain Tascallon, in which Cacama, Coanaco, Culcultza, Guatemozin, and sundry other gentlemen, whose names our pen is impotent to describe, ar mixed. ... Guatemozin taking offense at Montezuma's trucling to Cortez, stics his spear into him by way of sholng his displeasure. Teculllpo, the dauter of Montezuma, and also cousin and mistress of Guatemozin, does not like the action at all. ... The author possesses an imagination truly immense, a flo of language really Mississippian, but we fear that some mischievous genius has cut the string of his kite. No one can read the book without regretting that so much study and labor hav been so misapplied. The author must hav been laboring under a pressure of at least 40 pounds to the square inch, and a safety valve was a necessity." [Literary World. 500

FAIR GOD, The. [by Lew Wallace: Boston, Osgood, 1873; London, Warne, 1887.] "The name of Montezuma, now the symbol of a race and civilization dead and gone, is a name to conjure weird fancies with; and the court of that hapless monarch is surrounded with mystery and romance enuf to furnish material for a dozen novels. This work has evidently been prepared with care, and is written in a style which is captivating, if rather diffuse. But Gen. Wallace is so fine a writer that he sometimes groes tiresome. Besides, his novel has one great fault—prolixity." [Arcadian.]—"Far back in the dim twilight of the writer's history, he remembers to hav read a child's history of 'The Last of the Montezumas'; and the majestic yet pathetic figure of the aboriginal king made an ineffaceable impression on his mind. Whether from that dim memory or the more vivid one of Prescott's romantic history, we turn to Gen. Wallace's story with eager anticipation. Nor is it altogether disappointed. Montezuma and Guatamozin ar recognizable,—romantic heroes, types of that union of stern northern virtues with tropic softness and sentiment which in the story of conquered Mexico and Peru hav given such material to tragic art. And if one must go to medieval times, as has many a great writer, for the themes of romance, surely there is no more novel or inviting field than that dim era in the history of the New World when a handful of adventurers from a foreign land overthrew a mity empire with a civilisation older than theirs. The material is after Scott's heart. How majestically this pageantry of heroic figures would hav moved along his canvas! A greater rapidity of movement and greater clearness of pictured scenes, more dash and less inflation of style, and we should hav been very strongly reminded of the 'wizard of the north.' The story attempts the same picturesqueness and stateliness of style which Scott used facetiously to call 'the big bow-wow,' and in which he so wondrously excelled. And tho its heroics remind us oftener of Ossian than of Scott, it does not on the whole fail of dignity and eloquence." [Ladies' Repository.]—" It shows a great deal of industry and learning and power of description. From an artistic point of vue it is something between a panorama and a puppet-sho; but those who find Prescott's Conquest of Mexico heavy reading may be glad to hav a popular edition of it in novel form, and to them we can safely recommend it. The curious thing about the book is that it is full of invention and quite devoid of imagination." [Saturday Review. 565

BY RIGHT OF CONQUEST. [by G: Alfred Henty (1832-): Blackie, 1890.] "It is decidedly daring to introduce an English boy in Mexico during the triumphant invasion of Cortez, but the thing is not incredible, and Roger Hawkshaw is the most promising of heroes when he sets sail from Plymouth for the West Indies, and is wrecked on the coast of Central America. He makes his way to Tabasco, and finds himself eventually in Tezcuco, where he is regally entertained. 'Was ever an English boy in so strange a strait as mine?' he asks. 'What an extraordinary people! Gold seems as plentiful with them as common pottery with us.' Tho he does not become cacique, the Aztec king Cacama offers the hand of his sister to him, and he eventually marries the lovely Amenche, and goes home laden with wealth. But long before this happy event he endures not a little calamity and abundant fiting under Cortez. Prescott's brilliant work has of course supplied the author with the richest material of romantic history, yet it must be admitted that his skil has never been more convincingly displayed than in this admirable and ingenious story." [Saturday Review. 570

MONTEZUMA'S DAUGHTER. [by H: Rider Haggard (1856-): Longman, 1893.] "The reader is frankly informed, in the preface, of the short and easy way of dealing with Mexican history which the author has adopted. 'The more unpronounceable of the Aztec names ar shortened in many instances out of consideration for the patience of the reader.' This leads to the comic and almost irreverent effect of having Popocatepetl reduced to 'Popo,' and Huitzelcoatl familiarly addressed as 'Huitzel,' etc. In all this we suspect that Mr. Haggard too surely anticipated the determination of his public to reduce history to the point of suppression; to historical realism, in fact, his latest story can make no pretence, the commonplaces of Prescott being set off by impossible Spanish names and localities, spelled out of all recognition. But this, of course, is only the framework which the conventionalities of art make necessary, if inconvenient, for Mr. Haggard's customary mélange of adventure, love, fate, revenge and death. He puts it all into the mouth of a garrulous nonagenarian, whose long-drawn reminiscences prolong the thrills and the suspense in a way that can only be described as lazily luxurious." [Critic.

As collateral reading may be mentioned:—

MONTEZUMA. [by E: Eggleston: N. Y., Dodd, 1880.] " Montezuma was a Redman in the strict sense of the term, but a hero of a different type from the Red Jacket, Brant, and Pocahontas. In classing Montezuma with these he tacitly accepts Morgan's vue, that the Mexicans wer but more advanced Redmen; we ar surprised, therefore, to find here the old vue of the character of the Mexican empire as an absolute monarchy, with a court of great splendor and elaborate ceremonial. This notion we supposed had been completely disposed of by Morgan and Bandelier. It is important that our young people should not hav their minds preoccupied with false conceptions; and the true vue is certainly as picturesque as the false, and far more interesting. Apart from this we hav nothing but praise." [Nation. 575

MONTEZUMA'S DINNER, [by Lewis H. Morgan: in North Am. Review, April, 1876.] "Mr. Morgan in his paper goes over ground which is familiar to every child who has gloated over the fairy tales of the Spanish conquest in the pages of Robertson and his successors, and undertakes to sho that from the day when Cortez landed, to the day of the publication of Bancroft's 'Native Races,' there has been a total misconception and misrepresentation of the condition of civilization which the Spaniards found. Mr. Morgan approaches the subject as an ethnologist, and first asks, not what do the Spaniards, fond as they wer of bombast and extravagance, and anxious as they must hav been to magnify their exploits, say they found, but what was it antecedently possible that they could find there? If ethnology givs an answer to this question, we shal clearly be in a position to weigh the Spanish evidence and determin what part of it is probably true or what untrue. Now, ethnology does giv us the answer we need, for it explains that the Aztecs wer simply aborigines who had raised themselvs to a hier level of barbarism (not civilization) than other tribes; and that there is not the remotest possibility that they can hav had anything like a European court, with a king and nobles and retainers. The materials out of which the chroniclers hav constructed their marvelous tales of Montezuma's court wer simply these: A confederacy of tribes, with chiefs, living in communities, and having in each house one common meal. It is certainly creditable to the human imagination that on this slender superstructure should have been reared an edifice in which (we follo Bancroft) 'from sunrise to sunset ... 600 noblemen and gentlemen ... passed their time (in the antechambers) lounging and discussing the gossip of the day, in lo tones,' while the outer courts wer filled with 'retainers' to the number of 2000 or 3000; in which we find goblets of gold and silver, elaborate dinners made by 'cunning cooks,' chafing-dishes, '400 pages of noble birth,' a 'steward,' 'aged lords,' and a great quantity of other feudal properties and characters which would hav seemed to the democratic Aztecs rather out of place." [Nation. 580

THE SPANISH PIONEERS [by C: F. Lummis: McClurg, 1893] is "a series of sketches in which the part played by Spain in the discovery, occupation, and civilization of the New World is painted in somewhat vivid colors. . . . There ar few of us who hav an adequate conception of the heroism of the conquerors, the self-devotion of the missionaries, and the wisdom of the regulations of the Spanish authorities for the protection of the Redman and his elevation in the scale of humanity." [Nation. 585

YOUNG FOLKS' BOOK OF AMERICAN EXPLORERS. [by T: Wentworth Higginson: Lee, 1877.] "The hi praise awarded Mr. Higginson for the execution of his 'Y. F. History of the U. S.'

must be renewed for the idea of the present work. He has rightly conceived that the narrativ sources of history can be made as clear and as interesting to the youthful mind as 'Robinson Crusoe'; and happily the size of our continent and the fact that three nationalities took a leading part in its discovery and settlement, combine to giv a fascinating variety to the relations which ar available partly in the quaint English of the original, partly in that of Hakluyt and others, and partly in the sympathetic versions of modern scholars. Mr. Higginson's selections, which begin with the Norse discovery and end with the Puritans at Salem, hav been made with great discrimination, and often with a more subtle purpos than children, not on the lookout for historical 'side-lights,' wil discover on the first or on the twentieth reading. The field covered is surprisingly wide for the size of the volume. Columbus, the Cabots and Verrazzano, Cabeza de Vaca, Cartier, De Soto, Ribaut and Laudonnière, Sir Humphrey Gilbert, Capt. J: Smith, Champlain, Hudson, the Pilgrims and the Puritans appear in chronological sequence, telling their stories or celebrated by contemporaries and associates. Every book or chapter is introduced by a statement of the authorities quoted, and brief footnotes, not too numerous, explain the hard words and otherwise illustrate and correct the text." [Nation. 590

HEROES OF AMERICAN DISCOVERY [by "N. D'Anvers," i. e., Nancy R. E. (Meugens) Bell; Routledge, 1885] "contains enuf which is new and fresh to make it a genuin acquisition. The explorations of the Rocky Mountains form an important part of the work, but they come down only to Fremont's time; it would seem as if it might hav been better to omit Columbus and De Soto for the sake of including Major Powell and other later explorers." [Nation. 595

1542.

VASCONSELOS [by W: Gilmore Simms] deals with the adventures of De Soto in Florida. 600

LIFE OF DE SOTO. [by Lambert A. Wilmer: Phila'a, J. T. Loyd, 1858.] "This work exhibits research, and evinces a desire to tel the truth and to expose what is false and reprehensible. It is hardly strange, then, that the author presents De Soto to us not as a generous warrior, who made honorable conquests, but rather as a freebooter, whose chief object was plunder, and who perpetrated cruel and wanton atrocities; altho, compared to the butcher Pizarro, he was a model of manliness, justice and humanity. Many of the incidents ar related with great dramatic effect, and ar wel calculated to excite horror and indignation against the Spanish marauders. The account given by Mr. Wilmer of the capture and burning of the Peruvian Inca and the massacre of thousands of his subjects makes one's blood run cold." [Home Journal. 605

1562-68.

ATALA [by Fr. René A: de Chateaubriand: Paris, 1801; N. Y., Langley, 1844] is a "wel known and pleasing romance by the greatest of the modern sentimentalists. 'Atala' is scarcely an Indian tale, tho the scene is laid among the Creeks and Seminoles. It belongs to the school of 'Paul and Virginia.' Chateaubriand was too much of a Frenchman, and quite too great a sentimentalist to conceive the North American savage. The story is too little passionate—too tearful and tender—too fanciful, and, we may ad, too conventional, to lay the slitest claim to 'vraisemblance.' Had the scene been laid in Arcadia we should not hav quarreled with the legend. It is simply out of place and inappropriate. It possesses much graceful description, much which is picturesque and touching, impaired, however, by the wel known faults of the writer's style and genius." [Southern & Western Mag. 610

LILY AND THE TOTEM, The. [by W: Gilmore Simms (1806-70): N. Y., Scribner, 1850.] "By mingling, in due proportions, authentic records, legends, and appropriate fiction, the author has given to his countrymen a graphic account of the attempted colonization of Florida, Georgia, and South Carolina by the French Protestants, who, under the direction of the famous Admiral Coligny, sót there a safe retreat from the bitter hatred and unrelenting persecutions of Catherine de' Medeci. Beginning in 1562, the narrativ ends with the capture of the fortress of La Caroline, by the Chevalier de Gourgues, in 1568, when he avenged upon the Spaniards their atrocious conduct to his countrymen, Pedro Melendez having then beaten the Huguenots out of their settlements, and tarnished the honor of the Spanish nation by a series of massacres. But the purely historical parts of this book wil be those possessing least interest for the general reader. Its episodes ar its charm; and with them the volume is mainly filled. Very pleasantly has Mr. Simms interwoven facts and fancies, and contrived to giv prominence to the actions and the characters of individuals, without breaking the thread of his narrativ." [Albion. 615

FLAMINGO FEATHER, THE. [by Kirk Munroe: Harper, 1887.] The author has "made a charming story out of the romantic career of Réné de Veaux, that knightly young Huguenot who accompanied the Chevalier de Laudonnière on the expedition which founded Fort Caroline, and later became chief of the Alachuas, a tribe allied to the French. On the slender thread of tradition Mr. Munroe has strung a series of fascinating adventures. If he depicts the warlike deeds of those early days in a golden light and portrays the actors in them as possessed of almost superhuman sagacity, refinement, and chivalry, no one wil complain." [Boston "Literary World." 620

1607-19.

YOUTH OF THE OLD DOMINION, by S: Hopkins: Boston, Jewett, 1856. 625

COLONIAL BOY, A. [by Nellie (Blessing) Eyster: Lothrop, 1889.] "An old house in Frederick, full of antiquities, is the scene of the story, and there ar two heroes, a schoolboy of today and a lad, the son of one of the first settlers. The former discovers a diary of the latter, giving incidents in the history of the first few months of the colony. This diary, in which the author reproduces the spirit, tho hardly the quaint style of those days, cannot fail to awaken an interest in a somewhat unfamiliar part of our early annals. The best chapter, however, is that which describes an unexpected visit to Gen. and Mrs. Washington at Mt. Vernon, which is a charming piece of writing." [Nation. 630

1612.

MY LADY POKAHONTAS [by J: Esten Cooke (1830-86): Houghton, 1885] "is a very graceful and pleasing sketch of the Indian princess. It purports to be the tender recollections of one of Smith's companions, set down when old and garrulous in his English home. 'I who had lāfd at Smith for calling the blessed maiden his gardian angel, now bowed down before her, and, tho no vain and foolish Papist, but a good Puritan of Puritans, made her my Saint Pokahontas.' To say that the author has not succeeded in an archaic style is but another way of saying no one has unless it wer Thackeray. It makes but little difference, since the manner throughout is so agreeable and the handling now and then shows so true a poetic touch. By an admirable ingenuity, the notes which in fact supply the authorities ar so worded as to produce the effect that the page before us is a new and added corroboration to them, and not made from them." [Nation. 635

As collateral reading:—

CAPT. J: SMITH. [by C: Dudley Warner: Holt, 1881.] "The figure of Capt. Smith combines, in a rare degree, the qualities of picturesqueness and historic importance, and Mr. Warner, without shirking the historically important (and comparativly uninteresting) incidents in Smith's career, has a keen eye to the humorous side of them, and describes them with the intuitive skil of a humorist. His narrativ of Smith's American experiences rests, of course, on Mr. Deane's annotated edition of Smith's own accounts, which had already been systematically arranged, and to some extent popularized, by Prof. Henry Adams. But Mr. Warner's book wil, from its form, be read far more widely than Mr. Adams' article, for it humorizes, as wel as popularizes, the amusing tale of Smith's mendacity and Pocahontas' fame. He is also in a position to mention and to refute the rebutting evidence brôt in after Messrs. Deane and Adams' case was closed." [Nation. 640

LIFE OF J: SMITH [by C: Kittredge True: Cin'ti, Phillips, 1882] "may be recommended to those who wish this best class of books for boys—heroic biography. The story of Smith and Pocahontas, we notice, is told in the old way, with no intimation that it is a fable. It is all right to relate such stories, but the reader should be cautioned about them in a note." [Nation. 641

1614.

CHRISTIAN INDIAN, The. [New York, 1825.] "In 1614 Capt. Smith undertook a voyage of discovery and trade to New England, then called North Virginia. Our author supposes that he took with him, on this occasion, a young savage, called Tantum, who had some years before been carried to England. The voyage was unsuccessful, and accompanied with occasional skirmishes with the nativs. In one of them, a young Englishman was wounded and left for dead. He recovered, however, and is secreted by an old squaw. In her wigwam he is attended by a maiden who falls in love with him, and conducts him, throu many adventures, to a Dutch fort. Miona, the young woman, had been contracted to Tantum, who in some mysterious manner assists her in guiding and protecting the white man. Miona finally kils herself to protect the Englishman from some danger threatened by a prophet; and the story ends." [U. S. Lit. Gazette.]—According to catalog of Boston Pub. L'y, the scene of the story is Virginia. 645

TALES OF THE TIMES OF THE

EARLY SETTLEMENT OF NEW YORK: by J. F. Watson: N. Y., Collins, 1825, 214 p. 655

A HISTORY OF NEW YORK from the Beginning of the World to the end of the Dutch Dynasty, by Diedrich Knickerbocker. [by Washington Irving (1783-1859): 1809.] " To burlesque the pedantic lore displayed in certain American works, our historical sketch was to commence with the creation of the world; and we laid all kinds of works under contribution for trite citations, relevant or irrelevant, to giv it the proper air of learned research. . . Discarding all idea of a parody on the Picture of New York, I determined that what had been originally intended as an introductory sketch, should comprise the whole work, and form a comic history of the city. I accordingly molded the mass of citations and disquisitions into introductory chapters forming the first book; but it soon became evident to me that, like Robinson Crusoe with his boat, I had begun on too large a scale, and that, to launch my history successfully, I must reduce its proportions. I accordingly resolvd to confine it to the period of the Dutch domination, which, in its rise, progress and decline, presented that unity of subject required by classic rule. It was a period, also, at that time, almost a terra incognita in history. In fact, I was surprised to find how few of my fello-citizens wer aware that New York had ever been called New Amsterdam, or had heard of the names of the early Dutch governors, or cared a straw about their ancient Dutch progenitors. This, then, broke upon me as the poetic age of our city; poetic from its very obscurity; and open, like the early and obscure days of ancient Rome, to all the embellishments of heroic fiction. I hailed my nativ city as fortunate above all other American cities, in having an antiquity extending into the regions of doubt and fable; neither did I conceive I was committing any grievous historical sin in helping out the few facts I could collect in this remote and forgotten region with figments of my own brain, or in giving characteristic attributes to the few names connected with it which I might dig from oblivion. . . The main object of my work, in fact, had a bearing wide from the sober aim of history; but one which, I trust, wil meet with some indulgence from poetic minds. It was to embody the traditions of our city in an amusing form; to illustrate its local humors, customs and peculiarities; to clothe home scenes and places and familiar names with those imaginativ and whimsical associations so seldom met with in our new country, but which liv like charms and spels about the cities of the old world, binding the heart of the nativ inhabitant to his home. In this I hav reason to believe I hav in some measure succeeded. Before the appearance of my work the popular traditions of our city wer unrecorded; the peculiar and racy customs derived from our Dutch progenitors wer unnoticed, or adverted to with a sneer." [Preface to 1848 edition. 650

1620.

TWICE TOLD TALES. [by Nathaniel Hawthorne (1804-64): Boston, Amer. Stationers' Co., 1837.] " The author has wisely chosen his themes among the traditions of New England; the dusty legends of ' the good old colony times when we livd under a king.' This is the right material for story. It seems as natural to make tales out of old tum-bie-down traditions as canes and snuff-boxes out of old steeples or trees planted by great men. The puritanical times begin to look romantic in the future... Truly many quaint and curious customs, many comic scenes and strange adventures, many wild and wondrous things, fit for humorous tale and soft, pathetic story, lie all about us here in New England." [Longfellow in North Am. Review. 660

PICTURES OF THE OLDEN TIME. [by Edmund H. Sears: Boston, Crosby, 1857.] "As pictures of domestic life, colored by the passing events of the age, we must besto the blest praise on these tales. They sho that the author has studied the history of the various periods in which his scenes ar laid, with thoroness and accuracy. The hero of the first tale is R: Sayer of Colchester, and its scene is laid in England in the early years of the Reformation... The last tale presents a pleasing picture of domestic life in the Plymouth Colony soon after its settlement. The hero is also named R: Sayer, a grandson of the J: Bourchier Sayer of the second tale, and head of the Sears family, so widely scattered throughout Mass. The incidents of his life wer few; and the work of the imagination here is only to giv life and form to the details of a simple life. But even in this picture, we trace the hand of an artist in arranging and grouping his incidents. The sketch ends with an elaborate defence of the founders of the sister colony of Massachusetts Bay, to the great disadvantage of the latter." [Boston "Spectator." 665

STANDISH OF STANDISH. [by J.. (Goodwin) Austin (-1893): Houghton, 1890.] "In a prefatory note the author promises that this tale shal not mislead as to the stern facts of those far-away years when the Plymouth Colony was establishing itself in the midst of countless perils—albeit much of the romance woven around them is hers. And, in fact, if nothing else be gained from this book, at least a clearer light is thrown on all the persons and incidents of the time depicted. The delineation of Standish is everywhere strong and impressiv, particularly in the first description of his outward appearance, and in the tender farewel scene with Rose, his wife. Gov. Carver, too, is drawn with a sure and loving touch. Priscilla Molines, with her coquettish love of fun, and John Alden, 'the scholar,' ar, especially in the wel known love scene, very daintily treated. Altho the story can boast no plot, and no tantalizing social complications, it is wholesome and effectiv." [Nation.]—This is continued in "Betty Alden." 670

As collateral reading:—

TRUE STORIES FROM HISTORY AND BIOGRAPHY. [by Nathaniel Hawthorne (1804-64): Ticknor, 1851.] "This work consists of two parts—'Grandfather's Chair,' and 'Biographical Stories.' The first is devoted to a delightful conversational narrativ of the principal events in the history of New England, and the exquisit simplicity of the style is the beautiful medium of exciting incidents, characteristic portraiture, and just reflections... The genius of Hawthorne is visible throughout the book, and its ductility is evinced in the ease with which it is accommodated to the comprehension of young readers. In a simple, cosy, conversational manner he conveys the result of much study, thôt, and imaginativ life in the past; historical characters ar so represented that they b the reality of actual men and wome and the heroic and romantic in their natures ar delineated so completely in the narrativ of their actions, that the reader unconsciously builds their characters in his own imagination, and finds at the end that he has living and distinct ideas of persons who wer before mere names and shadowy abstractions." [Graham's Mag. 675

1621, March 22.
RUTH EMSLEY, a tale of the Virginia massacre, by W: H. Carpenter, Phil'a, Hart, 1850. 680

1625.
MERRY MOUNT. [by J: Lothrop Motley: Boston, Munroe, 1849.] "The greater part of the characters ar historical. Morton, the merry Lord of Merry Mount, fares better in the hands of the novelist than he does in the narrative of the stern Puritans, who looked upon him as a cantankerous roysterer, and not as a subject for picturesque delineation. There is much curious historical matter in Merry Mount, which wil be likely to giv it a more deeply interesting character in Massachusetts than it wil hav for other readers." [Holden's Mag.]—" Its merits consist in vividly reproducing to the imagination a period which even the driest annalists hav hardly touched. The novel might with propriety be called 'The Cavaliers in Massachusetts,' for its originality, as an American story, consists in bringing together Cavalier and Roundhead on New England ground. The hero is a loose, licentious, scheming, good-natured, and good-for-nothing English 'gentleman,' engaged in a project to outwit the Puritans, and to obtain the ascendancy in Massachusetts of a different code of principles and a different kind of government from those which the Puritans aimed to establish. Connected with this recless Cavalier is a deeper plotter, Sir Christopher Gardiner, pursuing schemes of empire and schemes of seduction with equal ingenuity and equal il-success. These two, with the folloers and liegemen of Morton—a gang of ferocities, rascalities and un-moralities from London taverns—constitute the chief carnal ingredients of the novel. Opposed to these we hav lifelike portraits of Standish, Endicott, Winthrop, and other Puritan celebrities, with only an occasional vue of the Redmen. The business of the affections is principally transacted by two persons—a pure, elovated, large-hearted and hi-spirited woman, and a noble-minded but somewhat irascible man; and this portion of the novel has the ecstasies and agonies which ar appropriate to the subject." [Graham's Mag. 685

1630.
HOBOMOK [by Lydia Maria (Francis) Child (1802-80): Boston, 1824] "is a brief and simple story, sketching our ancestors' manners, character, and circumstances with equal truth and spirit,—connecting with chain of supposed events, many interesting traditions, and exhibiting the author's talent in many passages of power and beauty. The style does not indicate the practised writer; stil, with many faults, there is a kind of graceful wildness which almost redeems them. The scene is laid in Boston, Salem and Plymouth, the tale relates to the earliest infancy of these colonies, and the principal characters bear historical and venerable names." [U. S. Lit. Gazette, 1824.]— "The principal characters, including Gov. Endicott, Lady Arabella Johnson and her husband, ar generally wel con-

ceived and supported; the sketches of society and manners ar drawn with a faithful hand; the incidents ar detailed with a truth and spirit which give animation and interest to the story. The author has an eye for the beautiful and sublime of external nature, and a heart for the tender and generous traits of human character. . . . A hi-born and delicate female, on the supposed death of her lover, has in a fit of despondency offered herself as the wife of a savage chief. She livs with him 3 years, at the end of which time her white lover returns; her copper one, with great magnanimity, relinquishes her and departs, and she is married to the former. . . . The tone of the work is generally sombre and accords wel with our associations with the early history of New England, and the days of sicness, sorro, privation, and religious austerity. We never read the record of those times without a sensation of melancholy and pity, mingled with respect and national pride, and the author of Hobomok seems to feel and inspire a similar sensation." [North Am. Review. 690

GRANDFATHER'S CHAIR. [by Nath. Hawthorne: Boston, E. P. Peabody, 1840.] "The subjects of the stories ar Lady Arabella Johnson, Endicott's adventure with the Red Cross, Roger Williams, the Pine-tree Shillings, the Quaker persecution, the missionary enterprise of Eliot, and Phips' romantic adventure in recovering the sunken treasure. . . . The stories ar beautifully told, in that pure, graceful, translucent English which has given the author so hi a rank, and with a vein of sound reflection, elevated moral feeling, and, here and there, a touch of quiet humor." [North Am. Review. 695

HOPE LESLIE. [by Catherine Maria Sedgwick (1789-1867): N. Y., 1827.] "Tho a multitude of attempts hav been made, 'Hope Leslie' is the only really successful novel which we remember founded on the early history of Mass. Even here, however, the writer has judiciously kept the historical element quite in the bacground, nearly all the incidents and characters being imaginary. The most interesting personage, Magawisca, tho a charming conception, is an aboriginal maiden only in name. She is the poetical, but not historical child of the forest; she is Pocahontas transplanted to the North, and not having a drop of kindred blood with the copper-colored savage of our primitiv woods." [Fr. Bowen in North Am. Review.]—"We ar introduced to the family of Mr. Fletcher, a friend of Gov. Winthrop, who has settled near the infant village of Springfield. During the absence of the head of the family, they ar all, with the exception of his son Everell, murdered by the savages, a scene which the author describes with powerful effect." [North Am. Review. 700

BAY PATH, The. [by Josiah Gilbert Holland (1819-81): Putnam, 1857.] "The characters ar wel conceived and wel sustained, and the story, tho quiet and sober in its coloring, is interesting from beginning to end. The descriptions of scenery ar those of a careful observer, and the exhibition of opinions, dogmas, and religious differences, as they wer 2 centuries ago, shows that the author's sympathies ar large, generous, and catholic. The story has a perfect unity, and the attention of the reader is never diverted from its principal personages,—the families of Pynchon the magistrate, Moxon the minister, and Woodcock the rude and free outlaw. There is an adherence to facts in dealing with these personages somewhat closer than is usual in historical novels. The colonial records giv authority for most of the statements, and the assertion of the preface that the tale is only a 'section of history' is veracious." [North Amer. Review. 705

KNIGHT OF THE GOLDEN MELICE, The. [by J. T. White: Peterson, 1857.] New England. 710

—— SAME (" The White Chief "), N.Y., 1859. 711

1632-61.

CLAIBORNE THE REBEL. [by W. H. Carpenter: N. Y., Ferrett, 1846.] Maryland. 715

PILATE AND HEROD, by N. Harvey Stanley: Phil'a, Hooker, 1853. 720

1635.

FAWN OF THE PALE FACES, The [by J: P. Brace (1798-): Appleton, 1853] "is a hily interesting tale, told with great spirit and ability. It turns on the early love-jealousies, continued late in life, of two veteran cavaliers who convert the then existing wilderness of Hartford Co. into an arena for their strife and animosity. It is written in a serious vein; the strict disciplin and stern morality of our Puritan ancestors being wel supported, without being overdone." [Albion. 725

LOST HUNTER, The. [by J: T. Adams: N. Y., Doolady, 1860.] "The hero livs on a lonely island off Connecticut. The story is mingled with the life of the nativs. The descriptiv power of the writer is great, and not a few of the incidents ar of startling interest. The scenes ar in general hily romantic, and they ar described with picturesque vividness. Portraiture of character is not the author's forte, yet more than one of his characters wil be recognized as true types." [National Quart. Review. 730

BETTY ALDEN. [by J.. (Goodwin) Austin: Houghton, 1891.] "The story of the hardships and hi courage of the Plymouth colonists wil always be interesting, and the author has recalled to us the hi-born women and brave men who lent grace and dignity to the loiiest toil, and has given pleasant, homely pictures of the sedate merry-makings which relieved somewhat the strenuousness of the daily life of our forefathers." [Nation.]—This is a sequel to " Standish of Standish," and is continued in " A Nameless Nobleman." 735

1636.

PEEP AT THE PILGRIMS, A. [by Harriet V. (Foster) Cheney: Boston, 1824.] "The hi and resolvd characters of the leaders among our Pilgrim ancestors, the dangers they defied, the sufferings they endured, and their various adventures, whether peaceful or warlike, with their savage neighbors; their courage, zeal and piety, and even their weaknesses and foibles, afford abundant materials for the novelist and poet. Other sources of interest ar to be found in the habits, manners and superstitions of the aborigines; and characters of less importance than Massasoit, Sassacus, Philip of Mount Hope, or his martial kinswoman, hav figured with effect on the pages of romance. It may be objected that the habits of the first settlers wer of too grave and stern a character, and their lives a scene of hardships too unvaried, to admit that admixture of light and comic description which is demanded by the taste of the novel-reader of the present age. But it is not so. The adventurers wer not all stern enthusiasts nor rigid sectaries. The leaders, it is true, wer too often persecutors, as they had been exiles, for conscience' sake. But many of their followers sôt the shores of New England from other motivs. The 'res angusta domi,' the desire of gain, the love of novelty, or a truant disposition, impelled many to a land which was described as a second Dorado, or an earthly paradise. There wer among them knaves, who, doubtless, wer accompanied by 'the tools that they do work with.' . . . Major Atherton is soon introduced to Mr. Winslow, Mr. Bradford, and other worthies of the time, among whom is Captain Standish. At the house of Mr. Winslow he meets Peregrine White . . . he witnesses the two bloody attacs upon the Pequod entrenchments." [U. S. Lit. Gazette.

——— SAME (new ed.) Boston, Phillips, 1850. "Altho the title conveys the idea simply of a tale of the early days of Plymouth, yet the scene of action is by no means confined to its roc-bound coast, but changes to Salem, Boston, the Connecticut settlements, and 'New Amsterdam.' The quaint language of the characters is in exact keeping with the time, and the strait-laced ideas and scriptural sentences of the Puritans ar very humorously given. . . Miles Standish, Winslow, Vane, and Winthrop, the learned Cotton, the apostolic Eliot, and many more ar presented to the reader, and pass momentarily before his eyes as in an exhibition of phantasmagoria. In describing Manhattan, we regret to remark, our author has committed a great error. While adhering faithfully to history as far as the Puritans ar concerned, she has adopted Mr. Irving's humorous caricature of our Dutch ancestors as her type in painting the Manhattanese. So closely has this pseudo-history been adhered to as to amount almost to plagiarism, and this, in contrast with her fidelity toards the Puritans, renders the treatment of one portion of her story—however amusing it may be—almost inexcusable." [Literary World. 740

1641-45.

RIVALS OF ACADIA, The: [by Harriet V. (Foster) Cheney: Boston, Wells, 1827.] "The author has succeeded in interweaving, in a very agreeable manner, certain historical events with a tale of no ordinary interest. . . The historical parts relate to the dissensions of two celebrated French colonists, D'Aulnay and La Tour, between whom was divided the extensiv province of Acadia. D'Aulnay ruled the territory lying west of the St. Croix; but, dissatisfied with this allotment, he endeavored to dispossess La Tour of his district, situated east of that river. The former fixed his headquarters at a fort near the mouth of the Penobscot, the latter at St. John. The colonists of Massachusetts Bay did not openly favor either party, but evidently leaned to the side of La Tour, for no other reason, perhaps, than that he was professedly a Huguenot. . . La Tour on arriving at St. John learns that D'Aulnay, taking advantage of his absence, has appeared with his fleet before the fort and demanded its surrender; but, meeting a warm reception from Madame de la Tour who heroically assumed command in the absence of her husband, he was so far unsuccessful." [U. S. Lit. Gazette. 745

CONSTANCE OF ACADIA. [by E: Payson Tenney: Roberts, 1886.] "It is in a general way true that the value of human endeavor is in proportion to practical result, immediate or remote; yet many ar the lives beautiful, strong, altogether tragical for which this standard of judgment is inadequate and unfair.

Such a life was that of Constance (Bernon) La Tour. The author of 'Constance of Acadia' has brôt into a light which she wel can bear this woman who was great in herself, and great in her aims, rather than in temporary achievement or in permanent impression upon the cause and the country which wer hers. Her soul was passionately devoted to noble principles, her mind persistently self-directed toards hi issues; to hasten the establishment of a French Protestant state in Acadia, her body knew no weariness, her spirit no discouragement. Yet, practically speaking, she livd in vain. The Huguenots, whom she hoped and prayed might rise from the ruins of La Rochelle to set up their altars in the wilderness, never won any appreciable footing in Acadia. The mass of the early French settlers was Romanist; their posterity is priest-ridden. The savages among whom she labored incessantly wer ever more easily won by the miracle-working, painted puppets of the Jesuits than by good works coupled with tedious appeal to an invisible, unsymbolized God. The carnal, astute husband, whose spiritual welfare was dearer to her than wer his worldly honesty and honor, could be without inconvenience either Catholic or Protestant, servant of Louis or of Charles; could shift politics and religion as garments whenever the self-interest of Charles La Tour demanded a change. Little more than two centuries hav elapsd since she died on the bastion of her forest fort, defending against Charnacé (the lover of her youth) her faith, her home and her handful of followers; yet on that very spot her name is but a vague memory, while to the world familiar with Jeanne Darc and the 'Maid of Saragossa' it is unknown. Clearly no page of history offers better opportunity for romantic and dramatic treatment as this. The events ar comprised in a few years, and ar fitted to the character of the actors as nicely as if devised by a cunning dramatist. The march of the tragedy is relentless, from the sacrifice of love for duty, made by Constance and C: de Menon (Charnacé) in Rochelle, till the tide of Fundy washes over Constance, and the body of the brilliant, subtle, spiritual French noble lies frozen by the shore. The strain of it is indeed so intense that one almost feels the final comic touch of the union of C: La Tour with the so-called wido of Charnacé to be a deliberate wile of the dramatist, intended to relieve the depression of his audience. . . The delineation of Constance, a much simpler, more defined nature, is more satisfactory, and that of La Tour is distinctly keen and admirable. There is room in him for a display of humor of which the author has a great deal, and of which he makes best use in the chapters describing La Tour's visit to Boston, and the Puritan debate in which a question of conscience was opposed to a question of cash down. But if throu technical inaptitude the author may fail to accomplish his expressed object—the popularization of colonial history—he has not shirked dry investigation, he has not lackèd feeling for his subject; and he has produced a work which may be read, and ôt to be widely read with both interest and profit." [Nation. 750

LADY OF FORT ST. JOHN, The. [by M.. (Hartwell) Catherwood (1847-): Houghton, 1892.] "Discontent with an author whose fictitious tragedy is weak is mild compared with that excited by the author who spoils an actual tragedy by surrounding it with fictitious circumstance. About five years ago there appeared an anonymous novel, entitled 'Constance of Acadia.' This book, tho defectiv in arrangement and style, shoed study and comprehension both of the details of the feud between C: La Tour and D'Aulnay de Charnizay and of contemporary New England history. The remarkable character and heroic life of Constance La Tour wer depicted with admirable fidelity and understanding. A second more or less fictitious version of this romantic but, in its results, insignificant, historical episode would seem superfluous, unless the person attempting it should be possessed of notable literary skill. Such justification is here not apparent. The fort, by the way, is historically and commonly known as Fort La Tour, or the 'habitation of the River St. John,' and the Lady as Constance, on which, either for sound or significance, Mrs. Catherwood's Marie is hardly an improvement. The events of the story immediately precede and comprise the surrender of the fort. Excepting a few particulars of the surrender, the book is unadulterated and commonplace fiction." [Nation. 755

THIRTY-NINE MEN FOR ONE WOMAN. [by H. Chevalier: N. Y., Braburn, 1862.] Canada. 760

1643.

NAMELESS NOBLEMAN, A [by J. (Goodwin) Austin (-1893): Boston, Osgood, 1881] " is full of improbabilities, but is in the main agreeably and intelligently written. The average novel-reader wil be apt to finish it, tho the climax comes long before the close, and after that the expedients to sustain interest ar rather weak. A young French baron, of the time of Louis XIV, is in love with his cousin Valerie, who, however, consents to wed his brother at the King's command. François thereupon abjures his nativ land and we next hear of him shipwrecked near Plymouth, Mass., and nursed throu a sicness by Mollie Wilder, a pretty and charmingly innocent young Puritan, who hides him in the attic of her father's house unknown to every one, and where he escapes the search for French prisoners (England and France being then at war) until his old Jesuit tutor rescues him. Before he leaves the house the priest marries him to Molly secretly, and when peace is declared he comes bac from Canada and claims her. The priest tries to prevent him from thus entangling himself with a peasant, and assures him that his service was only a hocuspocus invented for the occasion. François, however, is contemptuously immovable, and in the same spirit resists the importunities of Valérie, who, upon the death of her husband, returned to her first love, and crosses the ocean to try to win him bac." [Nation. 765

1650.

KONINGSMARKE. [by Ja. K. Paulding: N. Y., 1823.] Swedes on the Delaware. 770

1656-77.

VICTORIA [by Caroline Chesebro: N. Y., Derby, 1856]. New England. 775

EDITH [N. Y., Mason, 1856]. Quaker persecution in Mass. 780

TWO HUNDRED YEARS AGO [by T: B. Aldrich: in Cosmopolitan Art Journal, June, 1860]. Witchcraft in Salem. 785

NAOMI. [by Eliza (Buckminster) Lee: Boston, Crosby, 1848.] "We believe it to be faithful in its delineation of characters, and in its narrativ and incidents, to the reality of the past in our metropolis. Two dark epochs ar recorded in our history, clouding to some extent the noble and pure memorials of the fathers of New England,—the proceedings against the Quakers, involving fines, imprisonments, mutilations, banishments, and four executions on the gallows,—and the witchcraft delusion. Of neither of these tragical incidents had any writer availed himself in any considerable work of the imagination, or in an historic novel, til Mrs. Lee, in the volume before us, made the Quaker persecution the basis of her interesting tale. . . . The characters of the tale ar drawn with mingled delicacy and power of delineation; they ar true to nature and self-consistency. Beautiful sentiments and fine descriptions of scenery ar interspersed throu the volume, occurring at intervals as some relief from the contemplation of human infirmities. The ardent eulogists of the Puritans, who commend indiscriminately all which entered into their opinions and methods, wil doubtless take exception to what may seem harsh delineations of some of their sterner traits; but after all, the essential question is, ar they not faithfully represented in the garb of their age to us of this age? . . . The heroin presents to us an engaging and lofty character, with no weakness of sentimentalism or fanaticism to qualify our interest in her." [G: E. Ellis in Christian Examiner. 790

THE SCARLET LETTER, by N. Hawthorne: Boston, Ticknor, 1870; Chicago, Laird, 1892, Donohue, 1892; N. Y., Ivers, 1892, Burt, 1892, Ogilvie, 1892, Lupton, 1892, Munro, 1892, Lovell, 1892, Hurst, 1892. See No. 934. 795

PURITAN AND THE QUAKER, The [by Rebecca Gibbons Beach: Putnam, 1879] " is a story with a purpos—i. e., to rehabilitate the Quakers of colonial times, or, if it does not vaunt the discretion of the Quakers, to make clear the ferocious tyranny of the Puritans. If there is any one who believes that the Puritans came to New England solely or chiefly to find ' freedom to worship God,' this book may giv them [sic] a truer vision of the stern men who proposed to hav all things and people ordered as they saw fit, and undoubtedly called on the sword of the Lord and of Gideon to enforce their convictions." [Nation. 800

1660.

ROMANCE OF DOLLARD, The [by M.. (Hartwell) Catherwood (1847-): Century Co., 1890] describes the "exploit of 17 Frenchmen who, led by Dollard, or d' Aulac, saved the miserable French posts on the St. Lawrence from extermination by the Iroquois. The incident illustrates signally that recless bravery for which no men wer ever more distinguished than those nobles, priests and peasants of France who planted the fleur-de-lys and the cross side by side in the Canadian wilderness. The real story of the voluntary sacrifice of Dollard and his companions is simple, stern, heroic, in the hiest degree. It is told with full detail and deep tenderness, by Father de Casson, writing in Montreal a few years after the event. Mr. Parkman's English version leaves nothing to be desired for life and picturesqueness." [Nation.

PURITAN AND HIS DAUGHTER, The [by Ja. Kirke Paulding (1777-1860): N. Y., Scribner, 1849] " is founded on the adventures of a ' crop-eared ' enthusiast and his family, who wer compelled to take refuge in the New World. Here they pass throu various hardships and dangers, and hav divers encounters with the nativs. The heroin, however, suffers far less from these disasters than from an affection which had arisen between her and a young Virginian ' cavalier,' to indulge which they ar forbidden by the mutual prejudices of their fathers. At length the Puritan moves to New England; where, her father and mother having died, the heroin is accused as a witch and comes near suffering at the stake. She escapes, however; and difficulties being removed, finds a happy home in the Old Dominion." [Lit. American. 810

1661-85.

ROB OF THE BOWL [by J: Pendleton Kennedy (1795-1870): Carey, 1839, Putnam, 1854] "is an able work, which wil be read with pleasure everywhere; but to persons acquainted with the localities of the scenes described, or interested in the history of Maryland, the book wil bring a tenfold charm. The author's wel known power of description renders his account of the eventful scenes of the early colonists most life-like and pleasingly exact. The characteristics of the various personages ar also wel described, but a lac of power to impart a variety of manner to the several characters sadly impairs the vividness of the author's conceptions. The drunken trooper, Lord Baltimore, the fearless buccaneer, the silly landlord and his bonny dame, the gentle secretary and the Dutch ranger, all use the same quaint and stilted phraseology... The hero is a finely executed conception. The perfect originality of the design, the bold coloring and elaborate finish of this character, stamp the author as an artist of no ordinary power. The historical part of the story is wel carried out, and the struggles of the Lord Proprietary to maintain the Catholic ascendancy ar worked into the progress of the plot with skill and effect." [Gentleman's Mag.

1662.

BACHELOR OF SALAMANCA, The [by Le Sage: Phil'a, Hartley, 1868] "has one claim to attention upon the American scholar. It is evident that the second volume was written by some person conversant with Mexico under the viceregal government. The adventures purport to hav occurred in that country; the 'Bachelor' writes that he was a secretary in the palace. His statements, in addition, bear the authentic ring of genuin revelations. In an historical aspect, therefore, the romance is entitled to respect as a delineation of manners and habits. Don Lucas Alaman, the best of Mexican historians, believed his countrymen wer blessed under the Spanish crown. But the 'Bachelor' has thrown some dark shades into the picture, nor can the truth presented by his canvas be doubted." [Nation. 815

1664.

CONSTANCE AYLMER [by H.. Fitch, Parker (1827-74): Scribner, 1869] "here does for the early life of our colonies, Dutch and Puritan, and for the better types of American Quakerism as wel, what the author of the Schönberg-Cotta Family did for the Luther epoch in Germany. The 17th century at New Amsterdam, Gravesend, Breuklyn, and Eastward, is reproduced with that sort of naturalness and healthful treatment which marks the author of 'John Halifax,'—varied with threads of aboriginal story and character. Without being in the least sensational, the tale is full of incident, befitting those primitiv times, and avoiding every shade of sentimentalism, it is colored and made winning with healthful and noble feeling. A thoroly fresh and sweet book, which wil beguile many, we hope, by the loveliness and simple picturesqueness of the characters, and the charming naturalness of the narrativ, into sympathy with what is heartily pure and true, and a deeper interest in the genuin and grand souls whose lives lie underneath what we liv today." [Congregational Review.]—" The interest of the narrativ depends on its apt delineations of character, and the purity and sweetness of its style." [Hearth & Home. 820

1665-76.

TALES OF THE PURITANS. [by Delia Bacon: New Haven, Maltby, 1831.] One of these is 'The Regicides,' which presents, in very graceful narrativ, the legend of the 'White Lady of the Mist' who was supposed to hav some supernatural agency in supporting the regicides in their concealment within the cave of West Rock. We hav read the volume with great pleasure. The flight of these men, as a subject for fiction, offers an inviting theme to the novelist, despite all that has been written concerning it by various hands." [Southern Lit. Messenger, 1851. 825

1673.

THE FIRST OF THE KNICKERBOCKERS [by P: Hamilton Meyers: Putnam, 1848] "is a neat domestic narrativ of the days when the alternate rule of the Dutch and English, with the corresponding rotations of prosperity and office, afforded those changes of fortune which ar the best material for the novelist. Ad to this the effectiv grouping of Dutch repose and New England restlessness with the ruf bacground of the forest, and the stil ruffer characters of the sea who lurked in the province under strong suspicions of piracy and with undoubted evidences of wassailing, violence and terror, and you hav the chalk outline of the carefully wrōt picture presented." [Lit. World. 805

1675-76.

THE SPECTRE OF THE FOREST. or Annals of the Housatonic. [by Ja. McHenry: N. Y., 1823.] "The scene is Connecticut, and the manners of our Puritan ancestors ar intended to be described. The machinery of horror is far more various and complicated than in the Wilderness. We hav wars, Redmen, wild beasts, witches, trials, hangings, mobs, pirates, regicides, all conspiring against the reader's peace. . . The Spectre, who appears and disappears in a most astonishing manner on all great occasions, and constantly stands ready to help the author throu every difficulty, turns out to be no other than Goffe." [North Am. Review.

THE WEPT OF WISH-TON-WISH, by Ja. F. Cooper, 1829. 830

THE DOOMED CHIEF, by Daniel Pierce Thompson. 835

MOUNT HOPE. [by Gideon Hiram Hollister: Harper, 1851.] "The romantic history of the fugitiv regicides, Goffe and Whalley, who dodged the officers of Charles II. throu New England, is one of the most interesting episodes of our colonial history. We wonder that Cooper never acted upon the suggestion of Scott to bring these remarkable men before the reader and to embody in the form of romance the many poetic traditions which survive of their character and personal qualities. Mr. Hollister has attempted to do this, and the result has not been such as might hav been expected from the author of the Spy. Stil his book has decided merit. The title in itself is enuf to attract the reader's notice, as it is connected with the fate and fortunes of the most striking figure which stands out upon the canvas of those troublous days, when the redman was roused to a fearful revenge by the fraud and injustice of the whites." [Southern Lit. Messenger.]— "This is a story of Philip's War (1676) told by a writer who shows sufficient and faithful knoledge of the events of that war, and who enters ardently into the feeling of the men of those times. He has woven into it spirited pictures of the scenery of the places which wer memorable in the struggle. With some of these localities the author was himself familiar, and he has wrōt into his tale some of the stories which wer the delight and terror of his boyhood." [New Englander.]—" A spice of romance is given in the episode of Anne Willoughby, and a dash of the salt in the persons of sundry privateersmen and pirates; he serves it up to the public a very appetizing dish indeed. The various incidents ar well described and true to history, but the dialog is somewhat overstrained and unnatural. The appearance of Goffe at Hadley is much better given than in The Wept of Wish-ton-Wish, where the General is made to talk five mortal pages of nonsense while the Redskins ar making a rush of some 60 yards." [Literary World. 840

REGICIDE'S DAUGHTER, The, by W. H. Carpenter: Lippincott, 1851.

ROMANCE OF THE CHARTER OAK [by W: Seton: N. Y., O'Shea, 1871] " Is a picture of an eventful and interesting period in the early annals of Connecticut. The regicide, Goffe (†1679), Dr. Increase Mather (1639-1723) and other welknown characters, figure in the story. The Puritan spirit of the time and many of its peculiar social customs ar reproduced with fidelity and exactness." [Home Journal.

As collateral reading may be mentioned:—

THREE JUDGES, The. [by Israel P. Warren: N. Y., Warren, 1873.] " The Three Judges ar more commonly called the regicides, Goffe, Whalley, and Dixwell. Their history is comprised in the fact that they wer regicides, and became refugees. More fortunate than many of their associates who also livd beyond the Restoration, these three escaped the vengeance of the Royalists and obtained a refuge in the wilds of New England. After their arrival, their perils wer solely such as wer caused by their desire to linger about the settlements of their fello-men. In the wilderness they wer safe from Royalists, and hardly endangerd by savage foes. Yet as the sentiment of Puritan New England was favorable to them, these regicides livd and died in peace, known to a few friends, and only occasionally obliged to lie hid when some government emissary was in their neighborhood. Two of them, Gen. Whalley and his son-in-law Gen. Goffe, came to Boston at first without concealment; and the third, Dixwell, seems to hav livd undisturbed, with very little difficulty. The book is simply a repetition of the wel known facts in the case, giving undue credence to Stiles' collection of traditions about Goffe and Whalley." [Nation. 845

KING PHILIP'S WAR. [by R: Markham: Dodd, 1883.] " This was the last of the Indian wars in New England, and this book contains an account of all these, beginning, indeed—which was hardly necessary—with the Northmen and the Mayflower. The history is told in a very interesting way and may be recommended." [Nation. 850

DR. LE BARON AND HIS DAUGHTERS [by J.. (Goodwin) Austin: Houghton, 1891.] Dr. Le Baron is a physician of considerable importance who has two wives, and 15 or 16 dauters who marry and die throu almost every page of this exceedingly voluminous story. There is nothing in the career of any of them to build a tale upon, so what interest there is is centered in outsiders, who ar introduced from time to time without any apparent reason. It is a dul, prosy book. [Critic.]—This is a sequel to A Nameless Nobleman." 855

CAVALIERS OF VIRGINIA, The [by W: A. Carruthers: Harper, 1835] "is founded on the local history of Virginia. The first characters, of any importance, to whom we ar introduced, ar Sir W: Berkeley, Frank Beverly, his nephew, and Virginia Fairfax, his niece. The nephew is in love with the niece, and is favored by the old folk; but she rather prefers the hero of the tale, who is no other than Nathaniel Bacon." [New Eng. Mag. 860

HANSFORD, A TALE OF BACON'S REBELLION [by Beverly St. G: Tucker, 1857] "is a story of the old-fashioned sort, interesting in the main, but so prim, unbending, and precise in manner as to be rather heavy." [Mrs. Stephens' New Monthly. 870

1677?

THE WATER WITCH, by Ja. F. Cooper: 1830. 865

1678.

LEAVES FROM MARGARET SMITH'S JOURNAL [by J: G. Whittier: Ticknor, 1849] "is a volume bringing to the eye with the vividness of reality the scenes and characters of a past age, and making us as familiar with them as if we had ridden by the side of Margaret in her journey from Boston to Newbury, and yet throu the whole book runs a vein of pure poetry, lending a consecrating light to scenes which might possess but little interest if actually observd. The quaint spelling undoubtedly ads to the illusion of its antiquity, but what makes it really seem old is its primitiv sentiment and bold delineations. Margaret is a most bewitching piece of saintliness, with the sweetness and purity of one of Jeremy Taylor's sermons, and as full of general humanity as of beautiful devotion. Placed as she is amid the collision of opposite fanaticisms, the austere fanaticism of the Puritan and the vehement fanaticism of the Quaker, she shines both by her virtues and by contrast with the harsh qualities by which she is surrounded." [Graham's Mag.]— "The Diary of a Lady in New England, in 1678, had topics enuf for entry and reflection. There was the mixed provincial and European life, with the lowering, dusky background of the Indian and his forests; there was the reign of ecclesiastical rule, fatal to Quakers and witches, and drawing with it a train of fraud, fanaticism, and the numerous hypocrisies which overdone spiritual zeal reaps as a harvest; there wer the nicely drawn limits of domestic manners, an art of loving and marrying undreamed of by Ovidius; there was the simplicity of a rugged encounter with the soil or the sea for wealth yet uncreated—in fine, the most varied and abundant material for a novel by Scott or a history by Macaulay." [Literary World. 875

1684.

CASSIQUE OF KIAWAH, The [by W: Gilmore Simms (1806-70): N. Y., Redfield, 1859.] "The hero is a Sir E: Berkeley who purchases and settles a large tract of land in S. C. But the Cassique is not Mr. Simms' hero. It is his younger brother, a dashing Captain 'Calvert,' of the famous British cruiser, the Happy-go-Lucky, who had long been filing and pillaging the Spanish Dons, and finding in Charleston a sympathizing market for his plunder. Just about this time, however, the unscrupulous 'Merry Monarch' had sold himself to Spain, and the colonial authorities wer instructed to treat the bearer of the King's commission as a pirate. As this edict did not suit the interests of the Governor and of certain trading townsmen, the result was an equivocal position of ship, captain, and crew, which just suits a novelist's purposes—one especially who is familiar with the whereabouts of almost every scene. The semi-piratical, semi-mutinous privateers-men offer stil further opportunities; and to these may be added a glance at the curious social state of Charleston in those days. The romantic interest turns upon Captain Calvert having been cut out of his affianced bride in earlier days by his brother; and upon his having subsequently married a flirting, dancing, empty-headed, but lovely little Mexican, whose coquetry drives him almost crazy. . . Stil there is much of stirring movement in this tale; the phases of early provincial life and government ar striking in themselvs and wel developed. The fight with the Redmen is excellent." [Albion. 880

1685-1702.

REFUGEES, The. [by Arthur Conan Doyle: Harper, 1893.] "After having packed his Huguenots off the author launches into a series of romantic and exciting adventures, with the glory of leadership divided between a polished French soldier, Capt. de Catinat, and an ingenious son of the wilderness, Amos Green. Many of the incidents and descriptions ar derived almost literally from the Jesuit Relations. Mr. Doyle has made excellent selections from historical material wel adapted for romance, overfloing as it is with picturesque contrast of race and condition, and with instances of rare individual heroism. He has so much to tel that this half is a little hurried and breathless." [Nation.

STORY OF TONTY, The. [by M.. (Hartwell) Catherwood: Chicago, McClurg, 1890.] "The author is so occupied in working up fictitious passion of La Salle for the ascetic Jeanne Le Ber, and of Tonty for Miss Cavalier, that their passion for exploration of unknown lands—the passion which won them enduring fame—seems secondary and insignificant. No prominence is given by illustrativ incident to the great qualities of the two men, the irrepressibly initiativ spirit of the one and the resourceful loyalty of the other. Mrs. Catherwood even slights her avowed motiv, to pay honor to the memory of Tonty, whom she somewhat enthusiastically calls La Salle's 'great friend.' She has used very little of the material furnished by Tonty's authenticated narrativ, which is full of instances of his patience and courage in carrying out the designs of his leader, and which offers the best and also the most romantic testimony to the capacity for friendship possessed by the man with the iron hand." [Nation. 885

1688-89.

NIX'S MATE. [by Rufus Dawes: N. Y., Colman, 1839.] Gov. Andros in Boston. 890

FAIR PURITAN. [by H: W: Herbert (1807-58): Lippincott, 1875.] The transcript of Boston society under Andros appears to be faithful to documentary evidence. [Home Journal. 885

DAYS AND WAYS OF THE COCKED HATS, The [by M. (Andrews) Denison: N. Y., Rollo, 1860] "has some good qualities. The style is generally simple and correct. The few instances of attempts at fine writing ar failures. The story, constructed without art, is yet not without interest. The characters ar not sufficiently individualized. The chief defect of the book, however, consists in the anachronisms which jar upon the reader of any taste or knoledge, meeting his eye at almost every page. To write effectivly a story of Boston life nearly two centuries ago, it is necessary to be saturated with the language and literature of the times. The adoption of a few quaint phrases of old fashion, the copying of a letter wherein the spelling is slightly changed, is not enuf. But a fair style, liveliness in narration, with a goodly share of the spirit of the olden time ar not inconsiderable merits." [Albion. 900

—— SAME ("The Lovers' Trials"). Peterson, 1865. 901

IN LEISLER'S TIMES. [by E. G. Brooks: Lothrop, 1889.] New York. 905

BEGUM'S DAUGHTER, The. [by Edwin Lassetter Bynner: Boston, Little, 1890.] "The clandestine love affair of the young aristocrat, Van Dorn, with Hester Leisler arouses a mild interest, but not until he begins to develop the character of Jacob Leisler and his political ambitions does the author sho his strength. No single episode in any modern historical novel is better told than this of the Leisler insurrection in New York; and the construction, from the bare facts of history, of a living, breathing Leisler is simply masterly. In the end we ar permitted to see the coarse, fanatical, brutal Leisler, as he saw himself when brôt face to face with a shameful death—a death in which legal justice was not identical with human justice. History may not justify Leisler, but Mr. Bynner, in his finishing touches, rouses a sympathy for him which puts history to scorn. Any one who may read 'The Begum's Daughter' wil retain a clear memory of the events which brôt about the insurrection, and a fair impression of all the people conspicuously engaged in it." [Nation. 910

1690.

YOUNG PATROON, The. [by Ph. H. Meyers: Putnam, 1849.] "It has the same traits of quiet humor and observation, carefulness of style, and ingenious tho not complex contrivance of plot. There is a love of the subject, a kindling over old Dutch manners and Manhattan antiquities, something in the vein of Paulding, which is not the less attractiv for the modesty and reserv with which everything is set forth." [Literary World. 915

1692.

SALEM WITCHCRAFT. [by ? Boston? 1810.] "Our domestic manners, the social and the moral influences which operate in retirement and in common intercourse, and the multitude of local peculiarities which form our distinctiv features upon the many-peopled earth, hav very seldom been happily exhibited in our literature. It is true that Irving, in his 'Knickerbocker,' 'Rip Van Winkle,' and 'The Legend of Sleepy Hollow,' has given, in inimitable burlesque, very natural, just and picturesque vues of one class of people; but they ar all ludicrous subjects, and do little toards forming a history of the diversities of passion, sentiment and behavior as they ar manifest in any of our little communities, detached as it wer from the great world. We hav seen but two attempts of this sort which merit any praise, a story called Salem Witchcraft, and Mr. Tyler's forgotten, and we fear, lost narrativ of The Algerine Captive, both of which relate to times long passed. Any future collector of our national tales would do wel to snatch these from oblivion, and to giv them that place among the memorials of other days which is due to the early and authentic historians of a country. We say the historians—we do not mean to rank the writers of these tales among the recorders of statutes and battles and party chronicles; but among those true historians which Dr. Moore says ar wanting to giv us just notions of what manner of men the ancient Greeks wer in their domestic affections and retired deportment." [Lit. & Sci. Repository. 920

WITCH OF NEW ENGLAND, The. [Phil'a, 1824.] "The story begins when the Puritans' ancestors had been established in New England more than half a century. The two heroes—E: Bradley and C: Chesterly, the first the son and the second the protégé of the Rev. Mr. Bradley—ar soon introduced. They learn from Uncas, a friendly savage, that Samoset, a hostil and ferocious chief, was violently in love with Edward's sister, Agnes, and had determind to carry her away from the family by force; the attempt is made, and is defeated by Charles; of course, the rescued and the deliverer soon find out that they ar in love with each other. There ar some pictures of the manners of the Redmen in peace and in war, and of the peculiarities which at that age prevaild among our fathers, which ar wel drawn, but the whole power of the author seems concentrated upon his witch—Annie Brown—who is a little of a dupe, and much of an impostor, and altogether an abandoned wretch;—much which relates to her is conceived and written with great force. The last chapter describes her trial and death, and they ar told wel. Many of the circumstances, particularly the statements of witnesses, ar historically true; scenes which we could not believe wer ever exhibited on earth but for the most distinct and positiv proof. [U. S. Literary Gazette. 925

DELUSION. [by Eliza (Buckminster) Lee: Boston, Hilliard, 1840.] "We hav read this tale founded on the witchcraft of the early days of New England, with deep interest. It is the work of a thötful mind, warmly alive to whatever is beautiful in nature and in human character and life. The writer has succeeded in what has proved so difficult—in throing a positiv charm over New England scenery and manners. [Christian Examiner. 930

SALEM BELLE, The. Boston, Tappan, 1842. 935

SOUTH MEADOWS. [by E. T. Disosway: Phil'a, Porter, 1874.] "'It is somewhat incomprehensible,' says the author, 'that the delusion of witchery, which carried such consternation into New England and·desolated so many homes nearly 200 years ago, should hav received so little attention at the hands of the writer of fiction.' We feel bound to say that we do not find it at all incomprehensible, and this is not because we think writers of fiction hav been so surprisingly wanting in judgment as this author would imply; for 'nearly 200 years' they hav been singularly fortunate, as a general thing, in avoiding a subject which really offers them very few advantages, and does not at all urgently demand their treatment. Without assuming that, if the occasion here offered to the romancer is really pressing, it would inevitably hav been improved before now, we may still argue that a writer like Hawthorne would hav been likely to seize such an opportunity if it had existed. That he made no attempt to seize it seems to imply the chec of an artistic instinct, that the witchcraft delusion, systematically considered as an historical episode, cannot yield satisfactory artistic results." [Nation. 940

MARTHA COREY. [by Constance Goddard Du Bois: McClurg, 1891.] "This tale of Salem witchcraft is by no means lacking in vigor. It begins in the mother-country, where liv the actors with whom the fatal thread of Martha Corey's life is interwoven. The heroin, joyous, independent, and walking by inner light, is a character against whom the spirit of the times in which she livd would naturally be opposed. It would seem, however, as if the Rev. Mr. Parris had already enuf to answer for in the terrible results arising from his religious fanaticism, the flame of which was fed, history hints, by personal malice; but in this story he is dyed a still deeper blac by being made the purloiner of the private papers of a chance traveling companion merely to obtain temporary power over a stranger... The style is somewhat amateurish, but vigor of plot and fertility of incident save it from being commonplace." [Nation. 945

CAPTAIN KYD; or the Wizard of the Sea. [by Jo. Holt Ingraham (1809-60): Harper, 1839; DeWitt, 1852.] "No one can read a work by this author without admiring his hi genius and regretting his execrable taste. Beautiful conceptions, which come of moments of true inspiration, ar so marred by bungling embodiment, and gloing descriptions, which warm the blood and quicken the fancy, ar so hedged in by villainous weird-doing and diabolical clap-trap, that when the whole work is compassed, one hardly knoes whether praise or blame of the workman should preponderate... The prominent personages besides 'the Kyd,' ar a young Irish nobleman, Kate Bellamont, the daunter and heiress of an earl, and Elpsy the sorceress. 'A rocky headland, which stretches boldly into the bosom of one of the lake-like bays which indent the southern shore of Ireland,' is the scene, in 1694... The second division of the story has its action among the burgers of New Amsterdam." [Hesperian. 950

RAMON, THE ROVER OF CUBA, the personal narrativ of that celebrated pirate. Boston, Richardson, 1829. 955

RED REVENGER, The, or the Pirate King of the Floridas, by "Ned Buntline"; (new ed.) Boston, Studley, 1886.

TREASURE ISLAND. [by Ro. L: Stevenson: Roberts, 1884.] "'Treasure Island' is near Savannah. Flint, a noted pirate, buries the money in a spot unknown to his crew. He dies and the chart he has made of the exact locality falls into the hands of Billy Jones, his first mate. The circumstances under which it passes from his possession into that of Jim Hawkins, the son of a tavern-keeper, and subsequently into the care of Dr. Livesay and Squire Trelawney, are graphically described in the opening chapters of the book. Squire Trelawney fits out a schooner for the recovery of the treasure." [Nation. 965

1708.

KING OF THE HURONS, The [by Ph. Hamilton Meyers: Putnam, 1849] "Is an excellent novel. The hero is the celebrated Baron de Montaigne, the representativ of the French crown in New France, about the beginning of the last century. The story is connected with the historical events of that period, and is full of thrilling adventures and interesting scenes." [Literary American. 970

1709-55.
SIMON GIRTY. [by N. J. Jones: Phil'a, Zieber, 1846]. Penn. 975

1714.
KNIGHTS OF THE HORSESHOE, The. [by W: A. Caruthers: Wetumpka, Ala., 1845, N. Y., Harper, 1882.] "The historical basis of this tale is found in the 'Tramontane Expedition' under Gov. Spotswood to explore the country beyond the Blue Ridge... After the return from their successful journey, they formed themselvs into an order which held solemn and splendid meetings in the Hall of the House of Burgesses. Their badge was a golden horseshoe with the motto, 'Sic juvat transcendere montes.' This is but an episode at the close of a long and somewhat heavy story, for which Cooper evidently furnished the model." [Nation. 980

1715.
YEMASSEE, The. [by W: Gilmore Simms (1806-70): Harper, 1835.] "The author has not introduced machinery which is impossible, actions which ar improbable, nor contradictory to the times, the people, nor the sense of his fiction. There is fulness of incident and intensity of feeling. His hero moves and acts under a vail of mystery; he achieves much, knoes more, is the author of peace and prosperity, marries happily, and proves to be of hi standing." [Albion. 983

THE QUADROON. [N. Y., Trow, 1852.] "To one wel read in our colonial history there could be no happier period selected than that which this tale embraces. The description of New York as it was, of the manners of the day, and the habits and prejudices of the citizens ar extremely interesting." [Literary World. 980

1728.
HIS GREAT SELF. [by "Marion Harland," i. e., M., Virginia (Hawes) Terhune: Warne, 8vo, pp. 355.] "It is pleasant to come upon a romance which has in it much of the fine old flavor which our ancestors loved. It is based on real history, as attested in some memoirs of a Virginian family of great quality and stateliness. Colonel Byrd is admirably described: a noble gentleman of fascinating manners and brilliant conversation, the pink of honor and hi principles, benevolent but severe, too much of a tyrant to brook the slitest contradiction. And when contradiction comes in the shape of his dauter's determination to marry her Catholic suitor he derogates from 'his great self' and stoops to treachery which is dishonor. The tone of these old-world Americans is charmingly given, especially the stateliness which masks the underlying human feelings so long as they ar in repose. Some good points ar thrown away, as when Caliban gets nothing out of his discovery that his foe is a smuggler. The secretary too, whose changed manner when he draws the Colonel into his power is excellent, should hav met a fate more dependent on his bad courses. There ar admirable dramatic touches scattered throu the book, as in the conversation by means of which Colonel Byrd draws off Lord Peterborough over the border

of his own grounds and then suddenly charges him with duplicity, and again in the scene of the race-course and in Caliban's venture on Evelyn's mission. The end flags somewhat. In a romance the lovers need not hav been kept finally apart, but here no doubt the author is hampered by her foundation of fact. We must be contented with the vividness of scene and character which she oes to the quaint old memoirs, and must accept the too sad and too probable ending. Miss Harland (sic) has given the full local coloring of scene and century, and has painted an admirable portrait of the courtly slave-owning Southerner, who is so picturesque a variant of the English aristocrat as he appeared in the days of Addison and Steele." [Birmingham Post 983

As collateral reading:—

COLONEL W: BYRD. [by Constance (Cary) Harrison: in Century Magazine, June, 1891.] An admirably written and illustrated article.

1732.

BLACKBEARD. [Harper, 1835.] "We ar introduced to the passengers on board a vessel, which left Amsterdam 4 July, 1732, for Philadelphia. . . The tale is not without underplot: there ar the loves of Madam Markham, Dr. Eastlake, and Bob Asterly: the villanies of Blackbeard—murder—moonlight—burglary—and a variety of other queer things. Some of the subordinate personages exhibit a little spirit, and there ar a few detached scenes in the book really worth reading. [New-Eng. Magazine. 985

1737.

SATANSTOE. [by Ja. Fenimore Cooper, N. Y., 1845.] "The time is from 1737 to 1776. Chainbearer, the second of the series, traces the family history throu the Revolution, and the last, The Red Skins, is a story of the present day. 'This book,' says the author in his preface, 'closes the series of the Littlepage manuscripts, which hav been given to the world as containing a fair account of the comparativ sacrifices of time, money and labor made respectively by the landlord and the tenants on a New York estate, together with the manner in which usages and opinions ar changing among us, and the causes of these changes.' These books, in which the most important practical truths ar stated, illustrated and enforced, in a manner equally familiar and powerful, wer received by the educated and right-minded with a degree of favor that shoed the soundness of the common mind beyond the crime-infected districts, and their influence wil ad to the evidences of the value of the novel as a means of upholding principles in art, literature, morals, and politics." [R. W. Griswold, 1846. 990

1740.

PENELOPE'S SUITORS [by Edwin Lassetter Bynner (-1893): Ticknor, 1887] "is a charming little story. Inseparably connected with the romance of colonial Massachusetts is that great name, Nathaniel Hawthorne. The day has not come when any but a man of exceptional courage or a fool wil attempt a tale of a Governor and the Province House. Mr. Bynner has been bold, but not reckless. He has avoided tragedy, even intensity, and has simply told in Mistress Penelope Pelham's own words why she threw over her young lover, E: Buckley, and wedded the Governor, R: Bellingham. In the writing of this short diary the author's cleverness is most evident, because the author is nowhere to be detected. Neither Mr. Bynner nor any other man appears in a line of it. Its innocence and unconscious cunning, its simplicity and skittishness, even its neat sarcasm, are all pure maidenly. Penelope knew that Madam Hibbins, the Governor's sister, was her enemy, and why. But not an insinuation of that knoledge escapes from her pen. She contents herself with pelting the good lady with small stones every night after she has said her prayers and got herself into a sufficiently pious state of mind truthfully to record the day's events and her opinions thereon." [Nation. 905

WOMAN OF SHAWMUT, A. [by Edmund Ja. Carpenter; Little & Brown, 1892.] "Ezekiel Bolt and Penelope Pelham, both reared in the sanctity, and using the language, of Massachusetts Puritanism, ar seen pliting their troth in the almost too daintily idyllic first chapter. But, Puritan as she is, Penelope is not proof against the tempter who offers her position and wealth. He takes the form of the ambitious and capable politician Bellingham, who rises hi enuf to fil the post of governor of the colony. Bellingham, to secure Penelope, destroys the happiness of the young Ezekiel, who is at this time his secretary, and who, broken-hearted, falls bac on the humble trade of fisherman. Bellingham and his wife, however, suffer for their treachery. They are never forgiven by their nebors, and they lose their family one after another. The tragedy of these three lives is, indeed, beautifully, and at the same time, simply told." [Spectator. 1000

1741.

AGNES SURRIAGE: [by Edwin Lassetter Bynner (-1893); Ticknor, 1887.] "There is a charm about this romance which engages the reader's sympathies at the outset. The story is the familiar one of Sir C: H: Frankland's love for a beautiful girl whom he first saw scrubbing the stairs in the inn at Marblehead. He bròt her to Boston, had her educated, made her his mistress, and finally married her ten years later in Lisbon, in performance of a vow that he would do so if he escaped from the great earthquake... Agnes is throughout an ideal character, with the one necessary limitation... But if the author does not always rise to the situation, his book is good, and possesses in a rare degree that quality of atmosphere of the period which is so difficult of attainment, in addition to an agreeable style, which is suitably stately, but never heavy." [Nation. 1005

1744-48.

DEERSLAYER, The. [by Ja. Fenimore Cooper (1789-1851): Phil'a, Lea. 1841.] "Leatherstocking's life conveys in some sort an epitome of American history during one of its most busy and decisiv periods. At first we find him a lonely young hunter in what was then the wilderness of New York. Ten or twelve years later he is playing his part manfully in the Old French War. After the close of the Revolution we meet him again on the same spot where he was first introduced to us; but now everything is changed. In 'The Deerslayer' the character of Judith seems to us the best drawn, and by far the most interesting female portrait in the author's works. The Pathfinder forms a second volume of the series, and is remarkable, even among its companions, for the force and distinctness of its pictures. For us the battle of Palo Alto and the storming of Monterey ar not more real and present to our minds than some of the scenes and characters of The Pathfinder, tho we hav not read it for nine years;—the little fort on the margin of Lake Ontario, the surrounding woods and waters, the veteran major in command, the treacherous Scotchman, the dogmatic old sailor, and the Pathfinder himself. Several of these scenes ar borrowed in part from 'The Memoirs of an American Lady'; but in borroing, Cooper has transmuted shados into substance. Mrs. Grant's facts hav an air of fiction, while Cooper's fiction wears the aspect of fact. It is easy to find fault with The Last of the Mohicans, but it is far from easy to rival or even approach its excellences. The book has the genuin flavor; it exhales the odors of the pine woods and the freshness of the mountain wind. Its dark and rugged scenery rises as distinct on the eye as the images of the painter's canvas, or rather as the reflection of Nature herself. But it is not as the mere rendering of material forms that these representations ar most bily to be esteemed. They ar instinct with life, with the very spirit of the wilderness; they breathe the sombre poetry of solitude and danger. The Pioneers, the fourth volume of the series, is, in several respects, the best of Cooper's works. Unlike some of its companions, it bears every mark of having been written from the results of personal experience; and, indeed, Cooper is wel known to hav drawn largely on the recollections of his earlier years in the composition of this novel. The characters ar full of vitality and truth. Leatherstocking, as he appears in the Pioneers, must certainly hav had his living original in some gaunt, gray-haired old woodsman, to whose stories of hunts and fights with the savages the author may hav listened in his boyhood with rapt ears, unconsciously garnering in memory the germs which time was to develop into a rich harvest." [North Amer. Review.]—" We think the style of Deerslayer more polished, and the description of natural scenery traced with greater grace of outline and freshness and transparency of coloring, than in any of Mr. Cooper's previous works; while the incidents follo each other with the close connection, the graphic power, and the effectiv brevity of a drama. The scene is hardly varied, and the narrativ occupies but five days. Indeed, all the characters and dialog might be transferred to the stage with very few alterations. On the waters of one of our loveliest inland lakes, long before civilization had reached western New York, Deerslayer and his friend Uncas become the protectors of two lonely women from the savages who lurk around its borders. Our hero is already the cool and unerring marksman whose feats subsequently delight us in Hawkeye. But he is more than this. He unconsciously possesses that undaunted bravery and that purity and truthfulness of nature which ar the elements of all true greatness and for which he is so eminent throughout the five acts of the drama which bears his name. A sincerity, childlike, yet stern, endears the young pale-face to us, and commands our fervent admiration." [New York Review.] 1010

1745-58.

ENGLISHMAN'S HAVEN. [by W. J. Gordon: Warne, 1892.] "The effectiv blending of history and fiction in this clever and spirited story of Louisbourg may be traced, in part, to the romantic nature of the historical material which is woven into the writer's very ingenious plot; but it is only just to acknoledge the admirable art Mr. Gordon reveals in his persuasiv and lifelike story. Very few boys, we suspect, hav heard of Louisbourg, and of that first expedition against that 'Key of Empire' by the New England colonists [1745], and of the second siege [1758], in which Amherst and Wolfe and Boscawen wer concerned. Mr. Gordon's exhilarating book deals with some of the strangest exploits and episodes in the history of the struggle for dominion in America between French and English, and both the deeds and the men who wrŏt them liv again in this vivacious story." [Saturday Review.

TWICE TAKEN [by C: W. Hall: Boston, Lee, 1867] deals with the same events. 1015

PATHFINDER, The. [by Ja. Fenimore Cooper, Lea, 1840.] "We hav read this work with an interest and a delight which we hav no terms to express. It is a true work of genius... These volumes wil renew and increase all the old admiration which the author's earlier works awakened. Then, too, the subject—the wild woods and waters of our country—the old border warfare—the Mingoes and Delawares—the reader's old acquaintance, Chingachgook, the Mohican chief—and last, but more than all, Natty Bumpo, the veritable Leatherstocking, with his long rifle, Killdeer, a personage more familiar, more vividly and truly real to our imaginations and affections than nineteen-twentieths of the living men of flesh and blood of our daily acquaintance. The Pathfinder of these volumes is Leatherstocking, in the prime of manhood, acting as a scout and guide for one of the English regiments garrisoned on the shores of Lake Ontario. He is here freshly and clearly before us, the same inimitable being, with all his individual traits, with absolute identity of person, just what he whom we knew so perfectly when he was introduced to us in the earlier and later periods of his life, should be at the age of forty. And the special charm of the whole is that we hav him in an entirely new light—Natty in love! and most admirably is he drawn. He is just what he should be in love, just what nobody but he could be. The conception and the execution ar perfect; and the whole representation is instinct with a pathos, a moral beauty and sublimity, equally touching and ennobling in its effect upon our mind. As to the rest, the peculiarities of Natty's most original character ar charmingly brot out by the contact into which he is thrown with a positiv and dogmatical old salt-water sailor, who had wandered up to the shores and upon the bosom of a thing so incomprehensible to him as a freshwater sea." [New York Review.]—"The work is wel written, and filled with incident... Natty Bumpo is a character that can never grow stale. He is one of nature's philosophers. There is a beautiful simplicity in his actions, and a fountain of fresh, free thot in his words which wil always excite emotion and interest." [Southern Lit. Mess. 1020

FAIRFAX. [by J: E. Cooke: N. Y., Carleton, 1868]. Shenandoah. 1025

CANADIANS OF OLD [by Ph. Aubert de Gaspé: Quebec, 1862, 1890] is "the only French Canadian fiction which is worth putting into English. The story has no particular merit, tho it has some dramatic situations and is fairly wel put together; but the book has a distinct value, expressed by the translator when he says that it preservs in lasting form the characteristic customs of early French Canadians, and by its faithful depiction of their sentiment, throes a strong light on the motivs and aspirations of the race." [Nation.

1754.

DUTCHMAN'S FIRESIDE, The [by Ja. Kirke Paulding: 1831] "is a domestic story. The scenes ar among the sources of the Hudson and on the borders of Lake Champlain. The characters ar natural, and possess much individuality. From the outset the reader feels as if he had a personal acquaintance with each of them. One of the most cleverly executed is a meddling little old Dutchman, Ariel Vancour, who with the best intentions is continually working mischief: an everyday sort of person, which I do not remember having seen so palpably embodied by any other author. The hero, Sybrandt Vancour, is educated in almost total seclusion, and finds himself, on the verge of manhood, a scholar, ignorant of the world. He is proud, sensitiv, and suspicious; unhappy, and a cause of unhappiness to all about him. His transformation is effected by the famous Sir W: Johnson, whom he accompanies on a campaign; and in the end, a self-confident and self-complacent gentleman, he marries a woman whom he had loved all the while, but whom his infirmities had previously rendered as wretched as himself. The work is marked througout with Mr. Paulding's quaint and peculiar humor, and it is a delightful picture of primitiv colonial life, varied with glimpses of the mimic court of the governor, where ladies figure in hoops and brocades, of the camp in the wilderness, and of the strategy of Indian warfare." [R. W. Griswold. 1025

1756.

BOW OF ORANGE RIBBON, The [by Amelia Edith (Huddleston) Barr: Dodd, 1887] "is all alive with sturdy Dutch men and women, and brilliantly set off with King George's soldiers. The antipathy of certain honest, godly Knickerbockers for the youthful English representativs of the flesh and the devil is discussed with a great deal of humor and vivacity, and the romance of the little Dutch maiden with the giddiest of the offenders is as sweet and natural as tale of true love, not always running smooth, can be. The atmosphere of the story is thoroly old-time, and, whether the separate pictures ar historically accurate or not, they make a pleasant combination. The end is happy, and that is pleasant, too, for to leave such whole-souled, friendly, nice people in permanent unhappiness would be positiv grief." [Nation.]—According to catalog of Boston Public Library, the time is 1775-83. 1027

1755.

EVANGELINE. [by H: Wadsworth Longfellow: Boston, 1847.] "If we reckon everything as we hav reckoned all the chief things, all never could hav made for these Acadian people the place which their name and story hold now among men; not if we thro in the sadness of their being dragged forth, 7000 of them, and sent away in ships—and thro in, too, the bitterness of their after lot. Tears dry full fast from off man's cheeks; and full as fast, almost, flits the remembrance of those who hav sorroed and those who hav suffered. Millions, in the course of time, of others much like these hav, by their foes, been treated much as these wer treated and neither we nor our nebors ar now going lingeringly, and full of thôt and feeling about them, over their ground long after. The truth is that these ar Longfellow's people, that ar liked and pitied and remembered, and for whose sake their land has been sôt out, and these two books (very unlike, indeed) and others doubtless hav been written. Whatever has been said against the putting of English words into hexameters, such as can be made of them, and against the lightness or cheapness of some of the thôt or wording of 'Evangeline,' that poem has made all the abiding interest and feeling about the Acadians. , The real people seem to hav been very much such as Longfellow has made the people of his poem; there is little history; there is no official record, and scarcely even any record, of the driving-out. He has brôt into his verse true names of old French dwellers in the land, and names of some who wer driven forth, and the traces that are and wil be sôt, and the memories that wil be called up, of the erewhile Acadians, in the hamlets and townships of Nova Scotia and New Brunswick, about the Basin of Minas and the Bay of Fundy, ar those of the people of Longfellow's 'Evangeline.' . . . Most people, when they desire to know the true history of Acadia, will be content to read Longfellow." [Nation.]—Commenting on this assertion, Parkman wrote: "If so, they will not find what they seek, but in its place a graceful and touching poem and a charming ideal picture. The author of the remark just quoted ads that 'the history of events is not always the history of humanity.' But the history of humanity, to be good for anything, must rest not on imagination but on truth." 1030

1755-59.

WILDERNESS, The: [by Ja. McHenry: N. Y., 1823, Phil'a, 1832.] "The great merit of this book is the originality of its plot. Gilbert Frazier, an emigrant from Ulster, who speaks a language we do not understand, settles on the bank of the Juniata, whence he is carried a prisoner to the Monongahela by a party of French and Redmen, and becomes acquainted with Aliquippa, queen of the Shawnees. . . Mr. Frazier takes charge of the infant dauter of a French officer and educates her as his. This young woman, in the midst of a howling wilderness, with no companions but savages and the family of an Irish bogtrotter, becomes polished and accomplished by the assistance of an aboriginal prophet, who teaches her to relish the English classics! In due time a lover appears, one C: Adderly, who engages in several skirmishes with the Redmen, and uniformly comes by the worse. After a while Col. Washington appears in Mr. Frazier's cabin, and is so smitten at first sight by the heroin that he can eat no supper, tho he has made a long day's march over the mountains. At the first opportunity he offers the lady his hand and is rejected. In the meantime Adderly is plunging into difficulties without number, but is constantly saved from the consequences of his folly and mismanagement by the prophet. . . The book is chiefly valuable for the light it throes upon characters which hav become historical. The nativ chief, the knavish trader, and stil more knavish Yankee, stand before us. We see them move, we hear them speak, and we ar constrained to acknoledge that they wer not such as we hav imagined. Braddock falls and dies like a true English gentleman, surly and brutally uncivil; Washington appears, not good and great and dignified, as lying orators and historians hav represented him, but such as, doubtless, he was, (for we hav great faith in Dr. M'Henry) weak and silly." [New Eng. Mag. 1035

OLD FORT DUQUESNE: a tale of the early toils, struggles and adventures of the first settlers at the Forks of the Ohio, Pittsburg. 1844. 1040

OLD FORT DUQUESNE. [by C: McKnight: Pittsburg, People's Monthly Pub. Co., 1874.] "The scene is laid in what is now Pittsburg, at the time of Braddock's defeat. The author puts in a claim for credit on the ground of having faithfully folloed history, and of having carefully studied accuracy of local detail, and we believe that he is entitled to credit on this account. But in filling in his framework with the details, he has produced a fearful and wonderful book. It is very comical to hear the young Pennsylvanians and Virginians and Englishmen of the last century talking the language of the Old Bowery Theatre, and to see the dime-novel Indian fights and the other adventures of the curious beings who serv as characters. Altogether, it is a book which a boy may, we suppose, be allowed to read, and which we make no doubt that he wil like if he is allowed to get at it; and we should think it might be of interest to the Pittsburger, and to the illiterate Pittsburger a source not only of pride but of entertainment and delight. But that it does more than sho its author to be a lover of Cooper and Pittsburg is what we wil not affirm." [Nation. 1045

1757.

LAST OF THE MOHICANS, The. [by Ja. Fenimore Cooper: 1838.] "Among books which wil always remain with everybody, 'The Last of the Mohicans' takes a foremost place. Who has forgotten Uncas, or Maqua le Subtil, or the stately and sententious Chingachgook, or above all, Hawkeye, most real of American creations of fancy, and real in so many aspects, as the Pathfinder, as Leatherstocking, as La Longue Carabine? Who has not Killdeer in an imaginary gun-rac. and hanging on a peg in the store-house of memory the blanket which the Delaware chief threw bac that he might display the tortoise on his breast to his ancient tribe? Who has not seen in air-drawn pictures the cavern, with the sassafras screen, behind which the 'Palefaces' lurked while the deadly fight raged between the Mohicans and the Mingoes, who had 'dared to set the print of their moccasins in the woods' which once owned the sway of the Delaware tribe; the grave of Cora, beneath the young pines; the dead Sagamore, attired in the full-dress of his tribe and rank, with the children of the Lenape listening for the lament of the stern old warrior, whose lips remain silent, as he looks his last on Uncas?" [Spectator.]—" In painting Indian scenes of still life, or in delineating the warrior and hunter, the battle or the chase, our novelist, as he is the first who seized upon subjects so full of interest for the romancer, so is he alone and unrivaled in this branch of his art. The forest, ocean, and camp constitute the legitimate empire of Mr. Cooper's genius. At his bidding the savage warrior, the fearless seaman, the gallant soldier move, speak and act with wonderful reality. . . . Cooper unfolded the mysteries of the pathless wilderness, snatched its nativ lords from the oblivion into which they wer sinking, and bade them liv, before the eyes of the admiring world, in all the poetry and romance of their characters. The magic of his pen has invested the forest with an interest such as genius can alone create; he has so portrayed the character of a primitiv people, who wer men until the contact of civilization made them brutes, that, when they shal at length liv only in the page of history, it is alone throu the inspired pen of the novelist that future ages wil most delight to contemplate their character. Both Scott and Cooper hav thrown an exaggerated poetic interest around the characters they most loved to draw;—the rude Hilander and the savage of the American wilds ar, perhaps, equally indebted to the imagination of the novelist for the peculiar charms with which they ar invested." [So. Lit. Messenger. 1047

TADEUSKUND: the last King of the Lenape, by N: Marcellus Hentz: Boston, Cummings, 1825. 1048

SARATOGA [W. P. Fetridge & Co., 1856] "wil remind the reader of Cooper. It is absorbing in interest. In descriptiv passages it is remarkably fine; but the invention of the author appears to hav exhausted itself upon the character of Wild Jake and the incidents appertaining to him. Around this character a wild fascination is thrown, but the author's genius never gets beyond him. In no other character is there any successful individuality. Brigham and McCary ar weak dilutions of Cooper's backwoodsmen; Catfoot and Joe we hav had over and over again; and the two young lady heroins ar exactly what Cooper's heroins always ar—very uninteresting, prosy, sedate, overwise young women. This is pretty much the case, also, with the hero, and one keeps wondering how anybody could fall in love with him, or he with anybody." [Mrs. Stephens' Mag. 1050

TICONDEROGA. by G: P. R. James: Harper, 1854. 1055

BRANDON. [by Osmond Tiffany: N. Y., Stanford, 1858.] The author "thôt that the manners and social life of the 'Old Dominion,' with the introduction of some of its celebrated characters in the early days of Washington, might prove acceptable to the reader; and, while looking into the history of the colonies 'a hundred years ago,' he was struc with the interest of the Canada campaign of 1759. The fascinating character of Gen. Wolfe, with his daring and successful assault, appeared to the author to offer a brilliant episode, and he has yet to learn that the events of that grand enterprise hav been hitherto embodied in the pages of prose fiction." [Preface. 1060

WITH WOLFE IN CANADA. [by G: Alfred Henty: Scribner, 1886.] "The hero, a lad of 17, is an aide of Washington in the Braddock expedition and a captain of scouts during the later operations on Lakes George and Champlain. In the last 100 pages only the story of the capture of Quebec by Wolfe is told, the young captain being the leader of the party first scaling the Hights of Abraham. The book is thoroly interesting, and wil giv the reader a good idea of the military events preceding the conquest of Canada." [Nation. 1065

HAVERHILL: [by James A. Jones: N. Y., 1831.] "In reading this work, we wer favorably struc with the power of the author in describing the scenes and events of his hero's youth and his graphic manner of depicting Jamaica. ... Wolfe gave him a commission, after which he suffered many of the hardships incident to love and war." [New Eng. Mag. 1070

WACOUSTA: Phil'a, Kay, 1833; N. Y., Dewitt, 1851. 1073

ALGONQUIN MAIDEN, The [by G. M. Adam and E. E. Wetherald; Montreal, Lovell, 1887.] Settlement of Upper Canada. 1075

RED ROVER, The. [by Ja. Fenimore Cooper: Phil'a, Carey, 1827.] "The opening scene is at Newport, on a day of mingled rejoicing and sorro at the capture of Quebec and the fall of Wolfe. A mysterious-looking vessel, reputed to be a slaver, is anchored in the outer harbor, and becomes an object of speculation to three individuals who ar early introduced." [North Am. Review. 1080

AGAMENTICUS. [by B: Parker Tenney; Lee & Shepard, 1878.] "It is not a novel, hardly even a story, but rather a succession of pictorial chapters upon the early colonial life in Maine, about the time of the French and Indian wars. In style it is scrappy, inconsequent, and at times so far from clear that the reader is puzzled to understand what the author aims to express. Nevertheless there ar some chapters of really admirable description, and the good minister and his family ar wel drawn, despite a lac of artistic finish." [Library Table. 1085

As collateral reading:—

MEMOIRS OF AN AMERICAN LADY [by A.. (McVicar) Grant " of Laggan "; N. Y., Dearborn, 1836, Appleton, 1845; Albany, Munsell, 1876] " is a book which delited our parents, and is sure to delight their children. Mrs. Grant ' of Laggan ' spent several years of her childhood in this country, returning in 1770, at the age of 15. The 'American lady' who is here described is Mrs. Schuyler of Albany, an aunt of Gen. Schuyler, a lady of great character and intelligence, in whose household the young Scotch girl was for some time on a very intimate footing. . . The first 43 chapters (out of 66) ar of a general nature, giving a lively sketch of society and manners among the Dutch families, and a somewhat detailed history of the Schuyler family. The rest of the volume describes the author's experiences, chiefly at Oswego, where her father's regiment was stationed, and afterwards at Albany. It is hard to say which ar the best chapters of the book, where all ar so good; yet the last seem the best, as narrating the author's adventures, which ar naturally more vivid in style than the general description of manners and customs which we find in the first chapters. But even in these there is abundance of entertaining matter—the description of the system of slavery which then prevailed, the accounts of the savages, the social intercourse of the young people, and the adventurous life of the young men." [Nation. 1090

1763-99.

QUADROON, The [by Jo. Holt Ingraham (1809-60): Harper, 1839, London, 1840] " is a violent story of fine clothes and fierce passions; its epoch, the possession of New Orleans by the Spaniards; its main idea, the wrongs and perils which beset one of those ilstarred beings who giv to the book its title. The author shows no shrinking or superfluous delicacy in the treatment of his subject." [Athenaeum. 1095

1764.

YOUTH OF JEFFERSON, The. [by J: Esten Cooke: N. Y., Redfield, 1854.] "A critic of the Sydney Smith order, i. e. a gentleman who, in imitation of the wit, will pass upon a work without reading it, might be at a loss to kno why the author has dubbed this little volume 'The Youth of Jefferson'—but if one take the pains to read it throu, he wil find that it properly wears the title. It abounds in genial, happy mirth. All its pages sparkle with good humor, and, at times, there is a decided bit which, wer it not for the full tide of humor which overfloes it, might be mistaken for wit. A chronicle of college scrapes can hardly fail to interest the lovers of fun, and those who ar in search of it and will follo the hero, Sir Asinus, in his racy adventures, the victim of politics and love, wil not fail to discover it. We speak within bounds in saying that we hav enjoyed such hearty lafs over the pages of this volume as wil, we confidently believe, lengthen out the span of our brief existence at least a quarter of a century." [So. Lit. Messenger. 1105

VIRGINIANS, The. [by W: Makepeace Thackeray: Harper, 1859.] "The fortunes of the 'Virginians,' lying both in the Old Dominion and across the water, form the center around which is set off a moving, shifting picture of colonial and old-country life. The manners of the time and the humors of its people ar held up with faithfulness of detail which only patient search into the long-past domestic and social life could hav secured. The marks of student-like work appear all along the text and even in the queer and entertaining illustrations which adorn it. Mere sketches as these ar, we would not spare them, for their quaint restoration of the old manners, dress, and places, but more for the sober truth which seems to hide under their funny grotesqueness." [Christian Examiner. 1110

GEORGE STALDEN. [by Edmund Lawrence: Remington, 1888.] "It is unfortunate for Mr. Lawrence that one so readily recalls 'The Virginians' while reading the memoirs of 'George Stalden.' Two books could hardly be more unlike; but the mere fact that the story —and the story is of course the chief part of the memoirs—is laid in the same time with Thackeray's induces one to make comparisons, and any modern novelist who invites a comparison with Thackeray is unfortunate. It makes no difference on what line the parallels ar drawn—whether it is the human interest awakened by the story, or the antiquarian interest evoked by the reproduction of a bygone time—they reach the same end, and one's conclusion remains the same. This all may be said, however, without preventing the possibility of praising Mr. Lawrence's work for its own sake. It is painstaking, even and scholarly. The slightly antiquated style is never obtrusiv, and has a certain quiet charm which helps a great deal toards making the book readable. It must be owned, tho, that without the style and the interest of the time—a period especially appealing to the sympathies of American readers—the simple adventures and simpler romance of George Stalden would prove very dry material for the average novel reader." [Nation. 1115

VIRGINIA COMEDIANS, The. [by J: Esten Cooke: Appleton, 1854, 1883.] "The reprint of 'The Virginia Comedians' brings out very distinctly the great difference between the novel of the first half of the century and the novel of to-day. No one would think of bestoing so much pains and such literary abilities upon a similar subject now. A crowd of personages hurry throu a succession of striking incidents, imagind to illustrate the splendor and picturesqueness of the old régime in Virginia on the eve of the Revolution." [Nation. 1120

1755-75.

OLD CROW NEST. [by Ro. F. Greeley: N. Y., Ward, 1846]. New York. 1125

ORLANDO CHESTER. [by Sylvanus Cobb, Jr. (new ed.) Boston, Studley, 1886]. Virginia. 1130

LAST OF THE FORESTERS. [by J: E. Cooke: N. Y., 1856]. Virginia. 1135

SUTHERLANDS, The. [by Miriam (Coles) Harris: N. Y., Carleton, 1862]. New York. 1140

FATAL MARRIAGE, The. [by Emma D. E. N. Southworth: Peterson, 1863]. Maryland. 1145

JUSTIN HARLEY. [by J: E. Cooke: Phil'a, Today Co., 1874]. Virginia. 1150

JOHNSON MANOR, The. [by Ja. Kent: Putnam, 1877.] 1155

VAN GELDER PAPERS, The. [Putnam, 1887.] "The author has just missed writing a very good book. In a series of stories ar given some of the legends which attached themselvs to the early Dutch and English settlers in Long Island. Most of these stories deal with what may be called the comic-supernatural legend, in which the ghosts of Captain Kidd and the old sea-rovers play a prominent part. In 'Obed Groot' we hav the conversion of a miser to more liberal ways, effected by a 'Wild Huntsman' and his ghostly pue, and the unfolding of the miser's former life to himself in a dream. When the author deals with the ruf life and customs of the settlers he appears thoroly to understand his subject, and therefore draws very natural and life-like portraits. The story of 'Derrick van Dam' is most amusing, and the description of the manner in which Teunis van Gelder revenges himself upon Ebenezer Cock is excellent." [Saturday Review. 1160

STAR AND THE CLOUD, The; or, a Daughter's Love. [by Azel Stevens Roe (-1886): N. Y., Derby, 1851.] "The scene is laid in New Jersey when the borders of the Delaware wer covered with large estates. Altho the book is not the production of an unpractised writer, there is a want of skill in the arrangement of the plot and carrying out of the incidents, but the characters ar wel drawn, possessing strong individuality, and the story is in itself an interesting one. There is a naturalness and freshness about the book which we admire, and many of the scenes ar attractiv from this very adherence to nature and simplicity of incident. The heroin, Carrie Leslie, is a lovely character, and the truth and devotion of a dauter's love is shown in her attachment to her father throu all his varying fortunes." [Mrs. Stephens' Mag. 1165

1768.

GREEN MOUNTAIN BOYS. [by Daniel Pierce Thompson (1793-1868): Montpelier, 1839.] "The folloing pages," writes the author, "ar intended to embody and illustrate a portion of the more romantic incidents which occurred in the early settlements of Vermont, with the use of but little more of fiction than was deemed sufficient to weave them together and impart to the tissue a connected interest. In doing this the author has ventured, for the sake of more unity of design, upon one or two anachronisms; or in other words, he has brôt together some incidents connected with the portions of the two periods embraced in the work, viz. the New York controversy and the Revolution. Other than this, he is sensible of no violations of historical truth... The events which took place in the settlement of Vermont, and especially in 1768-75, deserv a conspicuous place in what has been termed the romance of history. The situation in which the settlers found themselvs was one peculiarly calculated to arouse the individual feelings of men. They had derived the titles to their lands from patents issued by the governor of New Hampshire, to which province it was then generally understood their territory belonged. A claim to this territory, however, was soon set up by the government of New York, and in the course of time certain statesmen of the latter province, corruptly combining with influential land speculators, procured, by their intrigues, a decree establishing the Connecticut river as the boundary between the two belligerent provinces, and thus throing the whole of the disputed territory within the jurisdiction of New York. In a change of jurisdiction merely the settlers of 'the N. H. Grants' would doubtless hav peaceably acquiesced. But when the tribunals of New York decided this decree to hav a retrospectiv operation, so as to involv the titles of the lands, the voice of the indignant settlers unitedly rose from every part of the Mountains, in determind remonstrances. After vainly defending a few suits brót for the possession of their farms, they paid no further attention to the summonses to quit, and found their settlements invaded by their foes, attended by sheriffs, each with a large armed posse for a forcible ejection of the inhabitants, and surveyors with their assistants for laying out and locating the unoccupied territory. Having thus found that peaceable measures wer unavailing, the now aroused and determind settlers unanimously resolvd on resistance. An independent organization was accordingly established throughout the Grants, consisting of committees of safety, as they were termed, appointed to act as provisional courts for trying offenders, supervising the public concerns in their respectiv towns, while to defend the settlers from aggressions of the New York authorities, military associations wer formed, the members of which soon became generally known as 'Green Mountain Boys.' And altho the shedding of blood was generally avoided, yet punishment of some kind was sure to be promptly administered. These punishments wer various and singular—sometimes ingenious and läfable. The most common mode, however, consisted in the application of the beech rod, or the Beech Seal, as they wer pleased to term it, in allusion to the emblem of the great seal of New Hampshire, of which their parchment deeds probably bore the impress; while this novel method of applying it, they humorously contended, was but to confirm their old titles. In this spirited manner was the contest commenced and continued by the settlers; and altho armed forces wer several times sent into the Grants to aid the authorities in ejecting the inhabitants, and altho all the leaders wer indicted and outlawed as felons by the courts of New York, and proclamation after proclamation issued by the governor of that province, offering large rewards for the delivery of those marked for the punishment of death and teeming with denunciations against all those who should offer further resistance; yet so united wer the people, and so determined the character of their opposition, that their baffled antagonists wer never able to accomplish but the most insignificant results for their years of labor in endeavoring to effect a foothold in the territory of Vermont, while the whole controversy exhibited to the world the singular spectacle of a few thousand poor settlers, thinly scattered over a wilderness of a hundred miles in extent, successfully resisting for a series of years the authority of a province apparently determined on their subjugation, and possessing perhaps 50 times their population and resources." 1170

365. 4 THE MINISTER'S WOOING [by Harriet (Beecher) Stowe (1811–): N. Y., Derby, 1859] "Is in every respect a delightful novel. The scene is laid in Rhode Island, in the middle of the last century. Most of the characters wer Puritans, especially the heroin, Mary Scudder, a young lady of a clear head and stout heart. The celebrated Calvinistic preacher, Dr. Hopkins, boarded with Mary's mother, and the old fello—represented in the novel as an old bachelor (tho, in fact, he at that time was married and had six children)—fell in love with Mary, who was in love with an unconverted young sailor. This fello went to sea, and after he had been absent a long time, news came that his vessel had been wrecked and he lost. According to the Calvinistic theory, it was supposed that he had gone to perdition, at which idea, his mother, who knew him to be a good boy, tho not a church member, goes into intense agony. She does not argue against eternal perdition, or the perdition of all outside of the church, but her misery makes a strong impression on every mind; an impression not favorable to strict Calvinism, and therefore the book was bitterly denounced by some religious newspapers. Mrs. Scudder, a zealous church member and great admirer of Dr. Hopkins, insists that Mary shal marry him; and the poor girl, giving up her lover as lost, finally consents; but at the last moment her sailor boy comes back alive, and they get married. Dr. Hopkins was an enemy of slavery, which then existed in Rhode Island, and so the novel contains a little abolitionism. Aaron Burr is brôt in, and he is represented as trying to seduce a beautiful French woman, and almost succeeding. This, however, as wel as the whole book, is handled in the most delicate manner." [Hesperian.]—"It aims to present the mental and the external characteristics of a period, and this it accomplishes with notable success in the course of a story narrated with singular skil and power. It is, in its portraiture of character, its pictures of domestic scenes and social phases, and its skilful analysis of the moral and religious temperament of a community, that the great excellence of this work consists. With thoro appreciation does Mrs. Stowe portray the moral and religious condition of the popular mind. Theology then and there was so supreme in its control over the minds of men that the actual government, the power which directed the movements of society, was theocratic. And what a theology! Gloomy, terrible, hopeless, uncharitable, narro, soul-deforming, love-destroying, un-Christian; having no excellence in its working, save that great one, not peculiar to it, that it enjoined the rigid performance of duty. Against this system which has begun to crumble, but which some theologians assiduously seek to re-edify, Mrs. Stowe has directed an engine which wil aid largely in its inevitable demolition. She has represented it in all its monstrous deformity, and yet she has drawn her picture not with irreverent hands, altho on rare occasions she has

used, perhaps all unconsciously, a tinge of ridicule." [Albion.]—According to catalog of Boston Pub. L'y, the period described is that folloing the Revolution. 1175

REJECTED WIFE, The [by A.. Sophia (Winterbotham) Stephens: Phil'a, Peterson, 1863] "is a New England novel with Benedict Arnold for its villain, who appears here as domestic traitor before his public treason is consummated. There is a good conception of some of the sturdy traits of New England character; the story is full of incident and of interest." [Commonwealth. 1180

REBELS, The. [by Lydia Maria (Francis) Child (1802-80): Boston, 1825; new ed., Phillips, 1850.] "Captain Somerville, nephew of Gov. Hutchinson, arrives in Boston in 1765. . . There ar many other characters,—a part of them historical, some of whom bear their own names. The historical events of the day ar noticed. The principal objection we should make to this story is the mingling of the ordinary incidents of ordinary novels with the most interesting facts of our history. The adventures which befel Miss Fitzherbert would be difficult, almost to impossibility, anywhere; but when Boston is assigned them as a local habitation, they seem peculiarly unnatural. . . There is little pretension to wit; the jests of the jesting character,—who is no other than the celebrated Mather Byles,—ar traditional and ar not very humorously delivered. Stil there ar among its pages proofs that the author has no common mind. There ar beautiful descriptions of natural scenery, eloquent expositions of sentiment, and passages of true pathos." [U. S. Lit. Gazette. 1185

As collateral reading:—The account of Dr. Mather Byles, by Eliza Leslie, in Graham's Mag., Jan.-Feb., 1842. 1190

TRAITS OF THE TEAPARTY. [Harper, 1836.] Boston in 1774. 1195

As collateral reading to the novels of this period:—

HOMES OF AMERICA, The. [by Martha Joanna Reade (Nash) Lamb: Appleton, 1879.] "A running account of some old dwellings of celebrity is interspersed with anecdotes and historical allusions not without interest. The 'Colonial Period' and the 'Later Period' between them take up a little more than half the volume, and that half being not necessarily a mere reporter's account of the houses of 'our first citizens,' can really be read with much pleasure. The venerable and most interesting Phillipse manor-house, now the city-hall of Yonkers, but stil unaltered and unmodernized in the main; the Van Rensselaer manor-house at Albany, stil in the direct line of succession and stil perfect; Gunston Hall, Stratford House, and Mount Vernon, and a score of other curious old buildings North and South, ar mentioned. A chatty account of the men who built them, and the men most famous among those who livd in them, is the extent of the antiquarian study attempted. In the Latter period we find Mr. Jay's house at Katonah, and the Morris mansion at Morrisania; Alexander Hamilton's house, 'The Grange,' in New York, and Mr. Longfellow's house, 'somewhat bac from the village street.'" [Nation. 1200

STORIES OF PERSONS AND PLACES IN AMERICA [by H.. Ainslie Wright: Routledge, 1888] "is an attempt, by grouping sketches of historical events with descriptions of historical places as wel as pictures of manners and customs of the colonial days, to giv a comprehensiv vue." [Nation. 1205

YOUNG FOLKS' HISTORY OF BOSTON. [by Hezekiah Butterworth: Estes, 1881.] "The good points of this book ar its being brót down to the present time; its abundance of anecdote; its quotations from Boston poets; and its illustrations. Its defects ar a want of unity and proportion as wel as of accuracy; it is neither literary nor scholarly." [Nation. 1210

1775-81.

HENRY ST. JOHN, GENTLEMAN. [by J: Esten Cooke (1830-86): Harper, 1859.] The author "is notably free from that pretentious bombast which has been so wel styled spread-eagleism. It is true that the tale is not entirely built upon revolutionary incidents, and that altho it is historical it is discreetly made up of a good deal of love-making and miscellaneous adventure, and very little history. But still the revolutionary cast of the work is decided, and, whatever the prejudices of the reader, contributes greatly to its interest; for the author has mingled his elements with equal skil and discrimination. This book and the Virginian Comedians, to which it is a sort of sequel, present the most truthful picture of the society of colonial Virginia that literature has yet produced." [Albion. 1215

—— SAME ("Bonnybel Vane"), N. Y., 1883. 1220

WYANDOTTE [by Ja. Fenimore Cooper (1789-1851): Bentley, 1843] "describes the fortunes of Captain Willoughby and his family, who hav settled at the Knoll, a hilloc that rose out of the pond in the form of a little rocky iland. It is minutely described, but without fatiguing you, for every sentence and touch brings out a point of the tempting scene. The spot is also chosen by the settler, partly as being easily defended against any hostil attempt which the savages might meditate, being near the Susquehanna, and at that period on the outskirts of civilization. Our readers may guess from these hints that the fiction is one not only of much domestic interest but of exciting incident." [Monthly Review. 1225

1775, Apr. 19.

LIONEL LINCOLN: [by Ja. Fenimore Cooper (1789-1851): New York, 1825.] The hero, "a nativ of Boston, becoming entitled to an estate in England, sails for that country, leaving his wife and infant in the care of his Aunt, Mrs. Lechmere. In the same house is a young woman, whom he had seduced, previous to his marriage, and by whom he had also a son. On his return he finds his wife dead, and, what is worse, he is informed by his Aunt that she had been unfaithful, and this information is confirmed by the oath of the young woman, Abigail Pray. The motiv of the former in fabricating this story was by diminishing his sorro for the loss of his wife, to render him more susceptible to the charms of her dauter. The latter on her part hoped to regain her former hold on his affections. But instead of restoring Lincoln's cheerfulness, they unsettled his reason; and after various adventures, he becomes the tenant of a mad-house. After the lapse of some years, his legitimate son, Lionel, becomes an officer in the British service, and returns to Boston, a short time previous to the beginning of the war, accompanied by his father who had contrived to escape from his confinement. He is unknown, however, to his son, who has not seen him for 15 years. His lunacy is of a partial kind, and is not suspected, being partially shown by an extravagant zeal for liberty. The work opens with their arrival and a description of the town and harbor. The passengers wer hardly landed when they wer introduced to the knoledge of a person who makes a principal figure in the book. This half-witted Job is rescued from the soldiers by Major Lincoln, and proves, in the sequel, to be the son of the baronet by Abigail Pray. He conducts them both to the triangular warehouse in Dock Square, then serving as a refuge for his mother. She testifies some alarm at the sound of the baronet's voice, but does not recognize him, and he takes up his abode without ceremony in the warehouse. Major Lincoln is conducted to the house of Mrs. Lechmere, in Tremont Street, celebrated as the dwelling of Sir H: Vane. Here he is introduced to the principal females of the story, Cecil Dynevor, the grandchild of Mrs. Lechmere, and Agnes Danforth, her cousin; the latter, a bitter whig who regards him with some coolness. At Bunker Hill he receives a wound which confines him to his bed for many months. His love is no way diminished by the attentions of Cecil, during this period, and his marriage folloes hard upon his recovery. . . The peculiar state of the country and the feelings of the colonists; the night-march of the troops to Lexington and their disastrous retreat; the battle and storm of the Bunker Hill redoubt; and the circumstances of a besieged town, ar all described with force, feeling and spirit. In short, Mr. Cooper has selected, in this instance, a period and subject replete with interest and has done great justice to both. [U. S. Lit. Gazette. 1230

THE BLACK WATCH. [Phil'a, Carey, 1835.] Lake George. 1235

THE RANGERS. [by D. P. Thompson: new. ed., Boston, 1851.] Ethan Allen and Bennington. 1240

THE RANGERS, or the Tory's Daughter [by Dan. Pierce Thompson (1793-1868): Boston, Mussey, 1851] "is entirely free from the exaggerated tone and overstrained verbiage which ar too often the prominent characteristics of our historical novels. Our author attempts no lofty flights of fancy; he relates facts; and has succeeded in accomplishing the object at which he has aimed, a faithful account of the most interesting period of the history of Vermont." [Literary World.

ETHAN ALLEN, or the King's Men [N. Y., W. H. Graham, 1846] includes Burgoyne's surrender. 1245

THE CLIFFORD FAMILY, Harper, 1852. 1250

1775 Oct.

BURTON, or the Sieges [by Jo. Holt Ingraham (1809-60): Harper, 1838] "is beautifully written and full of deep interest. . . It contains portraitures of gay gallants, knightly and chivalric soldiers, and renowned generals; and it wil, also, interest all who can appreciate female loveliness. The scene is laid before the walls of Quebec. The death of Montgomery, and the elopement of Eugénie de Lisle, a nun of Sainte Therese, ar among the incidents. The scene of the latter part is in N. Y." [N. Y. Mirror. 1255

CARLETON [Phil'a, Lea, 1841.] " The style is strikingly correct, and its incidents and reflections never, even by accident, startle us into unpleasant excitement. With this peace-offering upon the shrine of the decorous, we take the liberty of throing the book out of the windo." [Graham's Mag. 1260

THE ROSE OF WISSAHICKON, by G: Lippard; Phil'a, Zieber, 1847. 1265

THE METEOR, a Sea Story: N. Y., Long, 1847. 1270

MARGARET MONCRIEFF. [by C: Burdett: N. Y., Derby, 1860.] "From 1780 to 1795, Mrs. Margaret Coghlan made no inconsiderable noise in England. In 1793 she published her memoirs. Mrs. Coghlan was the dauter of Major Moncrieffe of the British army. . . In the account of her youth she bursts into expressions of rapture for a young American officer with whom she had become enamored [tho then only fourteen]. She does not name him; but that officer was Major Burr. . . Burr perceived that she was an extraordinary young woman. Eccentric and volatil, but endowed with talents, natural as wel as acquired, of a peculiar character. Dwelling in the family of Gen. Putnam with her, and enjoying the opportunity of a close and intimate intercourse, at all times and on all occasions, he was enabled to judge of her qualifications. . . . Miss Moncrieffe, before she had reached her fourteenth year, was probably the victim of seduction. The language of her memoirs, when taken in connection with her deportment soon after her marriage, leaves but little room for doubt." [Life of Burr, by Davis, 1837.

1776 Aug.

CHRISTINE. [by J: H. Mancur: N. Y., Colyer, 1843.] "The scene is laid in Flatbush, which, with its quiet and peaceful settlers, is wel described. Christine, like Sleepy Hollow, has its Ichabod Crane, characters distinct, yet indisputably belonging to the same genus. The book treats the operations of the Continental and British armies." [Bro. Jonathan. 1275

1776 Dec. 26.

KATE AYLESFORD, by C: J. Peterson: Peterson, 1855. 1280

1777 Aug. 16.

ETHAN ALLEN, N. Y., 1846.

THE RANGERS, by D. P. Thompson, 1851.

1777 Sept. 11.

BLANCHE OF BRANDYWINE, by G: Lippard: Phil'a, 1845. 1285

1777 Oct. 7.

GRACE DUDLEY, or Arnold at Saratoga, by C: J. Peterson: Peterson, 1849. 1290

SARATOGA. [by Eliza Lanesford (Foster) Cushing: Boston, 1824.] "Major Courtland, in the British service, takes up his abode in the colonies. . . He accepts a commission in Burgoyne's army, which was then advancing into the colonies from the north. In the course of that disastrous campaign he is twice wounded, and his life as often saved by an American officer, Colonel Grahame. The heroin, the dauter of Major Courtland is brot into a state of contiguity [sic] with the hero, by her attendance on her wounded father, after the surrender at Saratoga." [U. S. Lit. Gazette. 1295

1777-78.

THE LONE DOVE. [Appleton, 1850.] "The story is interesting, and the characters varied and entertaining. The reader is introduced to Washington at Valley Forge. Continentalers (sic) and Royalists, country dames and city ladies, Indians and sailors, crowd the scene, imparting great variety, but some little

1778.

THE COQUETTE, or the History of Eliza Wharton [by Hannah Foster: Boston, Fetridge, 1855] "is founded upon facts, and is full of melancholy interest. Eliza Wharton, a young lady of uncommon beauty of person and intellectual capacity and attractiveness, is sót in marriage by a young clergyman; but his sober wooing is disturbed and frustrated by the brilliant conversation of Major Sandford, an officer, who ultimately ruins his victim, and at the same time destroys the peace of his own life. It is told in a series of letters passing among the characters of the book, after the manner of Richardson; and, altho written in the precise and formal style of New England three-quarters of a century ago, the story is developed with considerable skill." [Putnam's. 1300

OLD TOWN STORIES [by H. (B.) Stowe: Boston, 1869] tels the same story, but with wider variations. See No. 107. 1305

As collateral reading:—

THE ROMANCE OF THE ASSOCIATION. [by Caroline (Healy) Dall: Cambridge, Mass., Wilson, 1875.] The author "came into possession of some dozen or more letters written by E. Whitman, and decided that they would interest many who had heard of the heroin of a New England tragedy of the last century. Miss Whitman was a belle of Hartford, the dauter of Rev. E. W. Whitman. In 1778 she started for Boston, ostensibly to visit friends, but never arrived there; later it was found that she died in Danvers, having given birth to a dead child. Scandal was triumphant, as she had never confessed a marriage, tho to her newly-formed friends at Danvers the unknown always asserted that she was a wife. A Mrs. Foster wrót the facts and fancies into a novel, which had a great vogue, called, 'Eliza Wharton; or The Coquette.' As Miss Whitman had been betrothed to the Rev. Jo. Buckminster, and as Pierrepont Edwards [1750-1826] was pointed at as the father of the child, the story spread like wildfire." [Nation. 1310

THE HAUNTED WOOD, by E: S. Ellis, N. Y., Chapman, 1867. 1315

1778 Mar.-June.

MEREDITH, or the Mystery of the Meschinza. [Phil'a, 1831, 200 p.] The British in Phil'a. 1320

THE QUAKER SOLDIER. [by J: Richter Jones: Peterson, 1858.] "The history of the 'Conway Cabal' and the secret movements of some bi officials ar admirably told. The scenes of the book take place while the British ar in possession of Philadelphia, and embrace a series of vivid pictures of the times, invested with rich local coloring. The events leading to the battle of Germantown, and the battle, ar described with a fidelity which shows the author familiar with traditions of the time and with the whole ground. Besides these historical merits the work has the cardinal one of skilful delineation of character. The Philadelphia Quaker is portrayed to the life; and not less accurate and graphic is the Pennsylvania Dutchman." [Mrs. Stephens' Mag. 1325

1778 June.

THE BUTTONWOODS. Phil'a, Harmstead, 1849. 1330

THE MARKSMAN OF MONMOUTH, by Newton M. Curtis: Troy, 1849. 1335

THE SPUR OF MONMOUTH. [by

H: Morford: Phil'a, Claxton, 1876.] "Washington is one of the prominent characters, and is wel drawn. For tho rest there is a good deal to praise; the people talk naturally and less as one is apt to imagin one's ancestors talked, that is to say, as if they wer human beings and not pictures or graven images; and there is a good deal of amusement to be got from the minor characters. As the romantic story of Catharine Trafford and Colonel G: Vernon, opinions wil differ; all wil agree, however, that there is no lac of romance about it. Indian John is an accomplished hero of fiction. In a word, this is a novel of considerable ability, composed of cleverly drawn incidents, some of which ar really impressiv; it puts a period of the Revolution clearly before the readers, and wil serv to interest young readers, more especially, and by young readers is meant those boys who ar fresh from Cooper and Marryatt, and who wil find nothing to harm them here." [Atlantic. 1340

NEAR TO NATURE'S HEART. [by E: Payson Roe: New York, Dodd, Mead & Co., 1876.] "The minor characters ar the most nearly natural, and there is a good deal of humor in their conversations. Washington, of course, makes his appearance, but there is no humor in the account of him; he always comes forward with the classic composure he wears in his representations on the postage-stamps. In 'The Spur of Monmouth,' another story dealing with the same period, that great man receives different treatment. This novel purports to be made up from the traditions gathered from old soldiers, and the awkwardness of the conglomeration of detached scenes lends probability to what might wel be part of an author's plan of mystification. The separate chapters ar for the most part tolerably life-like, but whether the main plot of the story is true or not must be decided on some more trustworthy authority. Altho the novel lacs a coherent form, it givs what it is fair to presume is an accurate impression of the time. Both this book and that by Mr. Roe ar at their best when fiting has to be described, and 'The Spur of Monmouth' has no ulterior aim to serv. The battle is told at length by both writers, and the secular one disputes the tradition which puts a soberly-worded remonstrance into Washington's lips, and insinuates that language of the kind popular among those who fôt in Flanders was uttered by him on that day. Indeed, the same author goes further and brings into his work a most extraordinary love-story in which Washington plays an important part." [Nation. 1345

1778 July.

THE BETROTHED OF WYOMING: Phil'a, 1830. 1350

GREYSLAER [by C: Fenno Hoffman: Harper, 1840] "brings into vue Brant and his vicious son; but it comprises, also, love adventures of thrilling interest, and turns upon a forced marriage of the heroin." [Athenaeum.]—Scene is the Mohawk Valley. 1360

MAID OF THE VALLEY, by A. J. Herr: N. Y., Graham, 1847. 1365

REBELS AND TORIES, or the Blood of the Mohawk. [by Lawrence Labree (-1859): N. Y., Dewitt, 1851.] "With Rebels and Tories, British regulars and Yankee militia, squaws and medicinemen, and a few battles and murders properly mixed in, Mr. Labree has concocted a book which wil doubtless ad to his wel-known reputation." [Literary World.

FOREST TRAGEDY, The. [by "Grace Greenwood": Ticknor, 1856.] "The scene of the story is laid in Fort Stanwix and its neborhood; and the chief personages ar a young Frenchman and an old Oneida chief and his dauters." [Albion. 1375

MARY DERWENT [by A., Sophia (Winterbotham) Stephens: Peterson, 1858] "is historical in several of its personages and not a few of its incidents. The tory Butlers, Sir W: Johnson, Queen Esther of the Shawnees, Brant, and other familiar names, pass before us, having more or less to do with the story, which included the Wyoming Massacre. The real figures, indeed, and the actual events of those days and that locality, seem to adapt themselvs readily to the author's hand, and very cleverly does she avail herself of the material. Indian and Colonist and visitor from the old country come naturally into contact, amid scenes of such stirring interest that the writer of fiction has but to choose her threads and weave them. But Mrs. Stephens does more. Her genius is essentially a bustling one, and delights in a range of wildest improbabilities. Next to truthfulness and easy sequence, commend us to florid invention and dashing resources. These hav their charm too. You don't want every tale to be a 'Simple Story,' or every heroin to be an 'exile of Siberia.'" [Albion. 1380

THE DUTCH DOMINIE OF THE CATSKILLS [by D: Murdock: N. Y., Derby, 1861] is "a stirring and wel-constructed tale, the scene being laid in and in the Kaatskills. The Dutch element predominates, and this is one of its chief merits, despite the too frequent larding of the pages with scraps of the Holland tung, sometimes without a translation vouchsafed. The 'muscular Christianity' of Dominie Schuneman would gladden Mr. Kingsley's heart, and he might even fall in love with Elsie Schuyler, who became, we hope, the mother of many generations of Knickerbockers, seeing that poetic justice is in the end dealt out to her, as also to the hi-bred and romantic British damsel, Miss Clinton, whose abduction forms the groundwork for all that is purely personal in the story. The Dutch colors, we say, ar wel laid in; the British, the Redman and the Negro (for New York was a slave state in those days) ar after the wel-used type. The book, we say also, is full of lively incidents, wel planned and wel developed. There is one scene, the climax, the culmination, the last scene as it wer of the fifth act, which is so intensely sensational that Mr. Wallack's eye ot to be directed thitherward. A heroin ready to flit off to glory on an eagle's bac; retribution properly dealt on manifold offenders; love getting a foretaste of his dues; and all on a slab of roc a dozen feet square —what a chance for one of 'our first dramatists!'" [Albion. 1385

—— SAME ("The Royalist's Daughter") Phil'a, 1865. 1386

PAUL AND PERSIS, by C. (C.) Brush: Boston, 1883. 1390

IN THE VALLEY. [by Harold Frederic: Scribner, 1891.] The author "is to be congratulated on having worked a fresh [?] field for a novel, and upon having made not only a new, but a successful venture. . . The Dutch blood of the dwellers in the Mohawk Valley should amble with pleasure at Maj. Dowd Mauverensen's strictures upon the 'Boston talkers' who hav inflated themselvs into fame, and upon the English, 'the blood-letting ilanders, who wer murdering one another by tens of thousands all over England, nominally for a York or a Lancaster, but truly from the utter wantonness of the butcher's instinct, the while we Dutch wer discovering oil-painting and perfecting the noble craft of printing with types.' These wer only outbursts, however. The book is a wel composed picture of Revolutionary times in the Dutch homes, at the Patroon's manor-house, and among bullets and tomahawks. An excellent balance has been held between the lights and shades of this composition, and a clever vein runs throu it all of the honest Dutch Major's own personality, his fixity, his faithfulness, his round-eyed attitude toards the tangles of this mortal life. His love story is a very pretty one, and in fine it must be said that the book may boast the non-negativ merit in an historic novel of being nowhere a bore." [Nation. 1395

1779 Sept.

THE PILOT. [by Ja. Fenimore Cooper (1789-1851): N. Y., 1823.] "The scene is almost always on the ocean, and the principal characters ar seamen; of course a very large and valuable part of the book must lose much of its charm with those who hav no acquaintance with sea terms or sea manners. From this circumstance it may not be universally preferred to the Pioneers or the Spy; but we think it richer than either in passages of original and true humor, of genuin pathos, and of just and natural eloquence. The language is uniformly good, and suited in its character to the occasion, and few books exhibit more accurate and felicitous sketching of human character and conduct, or more graphic pictures of the beauty or terrors of inanimate nature. 'Long Tom' is perfectly original, and is drawn to the life. He is one of a class of men who ar peculiar, not merely to this country, but to a very small part of our country; who leave the little Iland, which cradled them among the waves, and wander over the ocean, until it is to them as a home, and dry land becomes a strange thing;—and his person, habits, tastes, and thôts ar portrayed with great power and success. The evolutions on shipboard in storm and danger, and the appearance of the sea, convulsed and foaming under the lash of the tempest, ar all described with the same remarkable skil and effect." [U. S. Lit. Gazette.]—" The character of Paul Jones is drawn to admiration. The description of his conduct, firm, confident, and collected, whilst guiding the vessel of Captain Munson throu the surrounding dangers, breasting the angry waters, now bounding over a little space of clear sea, and again almost within the dangerous fury of the breakers, evinces the pen of a master, and the whole picture is strong and natural." [N. Y. Mirror. 1400

PAUL JONES, by Allan Cunningham: Edin., Oliver; Phil'n, Carey, 1827. 1405

CAPTAIN PAUL, by Alex. Dumas: N. Y., Williams, 1847. 1410

—— SAME (" Paul Jones "), N. Y., 1853.

ISRAEL POTTER [by Herman Melville: Putnam, 1855] "is a downright good book. There is in it a masculin vigor, and even a certain fantastical ruggedness, which separate it from the herd of smoothly-written tales, and giv it, so to speak, a distinctness and raciness of flavor. The hero fôt at Bunker Hill, and was soon afterwards carried prisoner to England. He escaped, underwent all sorts of hardships, carried letters between Horne Tooke and Dr.

Franklin, and sailed under Paul Jones. Franklin and Paul Jones ar admirable sketches of character; but our author is on his especial element when he deals with the sea and its belongings. The fight between the Serapis and the Bonhomme Richard is a masterpiece of writing; albeit some may deem its imagery too fanciful and far-fetched. Perhaps it is—but it helps the description wonderfully." [Albion. 1415

PAUL JONES. [by Molly Elliot Seawell: Appleton, 1893.] "Thackeray's 'Denis Duval' never reached the promised description of the memorable encounter of the Bonhomme Richard as seen from the decs of the Serapis. All Americans hav regretted this, for the master's touch must have added new glory to the already world-wide fame of Commodore Jones. We can be wel content, however, with the spirited rehersal of the incidents enacted off Scarborough on Sept. 24, 1784 [sic], which is now presented by Molly Elliot Seawell, in her recently published story. A conscientious study of the sources of history has equipped this capable author for her task, which none wil gainsay was wel undertaken." [Critic. 1420

1780.

THE SPY. [by Ja. Fenimore Cooper (1789-1850): N. Y., 1821.] "The narrativ turns on the fortunes of Henry Wharton, a captain in the royal army, who imprudently visits his father's family at West Chester (the neutral ground) in disguise, and there falls into the hands of an American party under the command of Major Dunwoodie, his sister's lover and his own friend.' He is tried and condemned as a spy, but succeeds in making his escape by the assistance of Harvey Birch, the pedler, himself a British spy, and with the connivance of Washington, who, under the assumed character of Harper, had been an inmate at the house of Wharton's father at the time of the stolen visit, and was firmly convinced of the young man's innocent intentions. Harvey Birch, by whose mysterious agency every important incident in the book is more or less affected, tho a convicted spy of the enemy, with a price set upon his head, turns out in the sequel to hav been all along in secret the confidential and trusty agent of Washington. This finely conceived character, on whom the interest of the narrativ mainly depends, is not without historical foundation." [North Am. Review.]—" The conception of the Spy, as a character, was a noble one. A patriot in the humblest condition of life,—almost wholy motivless unless for his country,—enduring the persecutions of friends, the hate of enemies—doomed by both parties to the gallows—enduring all in secret, without a murmur,—without a word, when a word might hav saved him,—all for his country; and all, under the palsying conviction, not only that his country could not reward him, but that in all probability the secret of his patriotism must perish with him, and nothing survive but that obloquy under which he was still content to liv and labor. It does not lessen the value of such a novel, nor the ideal truth of such a conception, that such a character is not often to be found. It is sufficiently true if it wins our sympathies and commands our respect. This is always the purpose of the ideal, which, if it can effect such results, becomes at once a model and a reality. The character of the 'Spy' is not the only good one of the book. Lawton and Sitgreaves ar both good conceptions, tho rather exaggerated ones. Lawton was somewhat too burly a Virginian, and his appetite was too strong an ingredient in his chivalry." [W: G. Simms.]—'The Spy' "was not merely a triumph,—it was a revelation, for it showed that our society and history, young as they wer, could furnish characters and incidents for the most inviting form of romance. There was a truthfulness about it which everybody could feel. And yet there was a skilful grouping of characters, a happy contrast of situations and interests, an intermingling of grave and gay, of individual eccentricities and natural feeling, a life in the narrativ and a graphic power in the descriptions which, in spite of some commonplace, and some defects in the artistic arrangement of the plot, raised it, at once, to the first class among works of the imagination. But its peculiar characteristic, and to which it oes, above all others, its rank as a work of invention, was the character of Harvey Birch." [Homes of American Authors. 1425

1780 May.

THE BRAVO'S DAUGHTER. [by A. J. H. Duganne: N. Y., Stringer, 1840.] Siege of Charleston. 1430

THE PARTISAN [by W: Gilmore Simms (1806-70): Harper, 1838, Redfield, 1854] "is a historical romance of a hi character, dating from the fall of Charleston in 1780 [May 12], and presenting a picture of the condition, prospects and resources of the province during the struggle of Gates with Cornwallis. Gates, Marion, De Kalb, Cornwallis, Tarleton, and other names wel known to history ar among the chief personages, and the incidents ar drawn from history, from tradition, and from local chronicles. A work like this servs to impress upon the mind of the reader a living and abiding sense of the greatness of the struggle which made our country free, as no records of history alone could do." [Norton's Lit. Gazette. 1435

MARION'S MEN. Phil'a, Rockafellar, 1843. 1440

MARION AND HIS MEN. N. Y., Graham, 1846. 1445

MARION'S BRIGADE, by J: H. Robinson: [new ed.] Boston, Studley, 1886. 1450

1780 Aug. 10.

FREDERICK DE ALGEROY: [by "Giles Gazer": N. Y., Collins, 1825.] "If it wer not too despicable for serious notice, we should be tempted to treat parts of this book with extreme severity. It is calculated to hav a bad influence, if it has any; but we trust that the wretchedness of its execution will prevent its finding many readers." [U. S. Lit. Gazette. 1455

1780 Sept.

PEMBERTON. [by H: Peterson: Lippincott, 1873.] André, Honora Sneyd, Arnold, and Washington and his sweethearts play more or less important parts in this novel. The story has no more of exaggeration than is usual with so-called 'historical novels.' The style is sprightly, and we believe the book is adapted to please a large circle. It is not without wit, either. Hardly one novel in twenty is good enuf to praise heartily; and we dare say that Pemberton will suit many a reader much better than a more ambitious book." [Independent. 1460

MELLICHAMPE. [by W: Gilmore Simms.] "'The Partisan' [May-Aug., 1780] closed with the defeat of Gates at

Camden. 'Mellichampe' illustrated the interval between this event and the arrival of Greene with the rude material for the organization of a second army, and was more particularly intended to do honor to the resolute and hearty patriotism of the scattered bands of patriots who stil maintained a predatory warfare against the foe among the swamps and thickets, rather keeping alive the spirit of the country than operating decisively for its rescue. 'The Kinsman' occupied a third period, and when the wary policy of Greene began to make itself felt, in the gradual isolation and overthro of the detached posts which the enemy had established; while 'Katherine Walton,' closing the career of certain parties introduced in 'The Partisan,' and making complete the trilogy begun in that work, was designed to sho the fluctuations of the contest, the spirit with which it was carried on, and to embody certain events of great individual interest connected with the fortunes of persons not less distinguished by their individual worth of character, and their influences upon the general history, than by the romantic circumstances groing out of their career." [Criterion.]—'The Foragers' is the 5th of the series, 'Eutaw' being the 6th and last. 1465

THE KINSMAN [by W: G. Simms; Appleton, 1841] gives us " a plentiful allowance of the partisan warfare of the Revolution, with all the accompaniments bestoed upon it by inferior writers, such as horsemen galloping about with prodigious pertinency and no very definit object, but who always happen to bring up exactly in the spot where they ar most wanted; a hero who is always getting himself into scrapes, and as regularly helped out of them by a kind of bac-woods Mephistopheles; the whole embellished with a profusion of very opportune rifle shots from the piece of the aforesaid forester, sabre cuts, brawling, bullying, hanging, arson and robbery and such like 'agrémens.' We hope Mr. Simms, who is a man of decided ability, will make a better use of it in the future." [N. Y. Mirror. 1470

—— SAME (" The Scout "). 1471

KATHARINE WALTON. [by W: Gilmore Simms [new ed.]; N. Y., Redfield, 1859.] " We say of 'historical inquiry,' because the Revolutionary tales of Mr. Simms ar essentially histories. They contain a great number of lucidly detailed facts: more than one campaign is elaborately and faithfully narrated, as we find it in the more pretentious volumes of the regular historians; but this is only a small part of the historical value of the author's romances. They contain more than the mere facts—the skeletons, so to speak, of history; it is the warm, vividly colored picture which we see in his pages. The bare skeleton is clothed again with flesh and muscle, the blood courses to and fro throu the veins, the eyes flash, the lips move, the face gloes and thrills with the life and animation which characterized it in the past. We see the actual epoch in Mr. Simms' books; the Revolution is no longer a mere historic event—we ar shows what it really was, how it was conducted, what passions burned in the bosoms of the actors, and under how much pain and suffering the great deeds of our forefathers wer enacted; in the great battle, or the obscure skirmish; in known or unknown encounters; in the dark recesses of the swamp, as on the open field, before the eyes of all. The series of romances ar so many careful and elaborate 'studies' of the contest. It was plainly the author's intent to delineate the bitter struggle in South Carolina, throuout all its phases and from every point of vue. The result has been these volumes which ar a complete epitome of the entire epoch, with all its scenes, events, and actors, vividly drawn, instinct with life, and thrown upon the canvas with all the vigor and picturesque coloring of a master. In the Partisan, Mellichampe, Katharine Walton, The Scout, and Woodcraft, the design is regularly pursued; and the result has been a great historic panorama, filled with vivid interest, and no less replete with valuable instruction . . . His sympathies ar strongly in favor of vivid adventure and hazardous crises,—of 'disastrous chances,' 'hairbreadth 'scapes,' and 'moving accidents by flood and field.' His imagination, large, excitable and working with vehement strength whenever it is aroused, rejects the monotony and sameness of every-day life, the dul routine of our prosaic age. Having selected for his field of operation the hurrying and changeful scene of the Revolutionary era, Mr. Simms avails himself of every advantage attaching to the period and its modes of life; he embodies all the passion and humor and excitement of the tragedy or the tragicomedy; he rides with his troopers on the nocturnal foray; burrocs with Marion and his men in the swamps of the Santee, and catches everywhere the rush and roar of the contest, the entire spirit and meaning of the drama. So strong is this characteristic in some of these books that the reader is almost oppressed with the thronging incident, the plot within the plot, the never resting advance of the narrativ. . . We hazard nothing in saying that in delicate delineation of woman and the passion of 'heroic love,' to use old Burton's phrase, Mr. Simms is surpassed by no writer since the days of Walter Scott. It is really refreshing to leave for a time the society of the heartless and wicked women, whom many novelists delight in painting, and pass an hour or two with some one of the heroins in these stories. The change is wholesome —as it is always wholesome to pass from the company of bad and selfish people into that of the pure and good. There is about the characters and emotions of the young ladies delineated by Mr. Simms a purity, freshness, and artless goodness which is extremely delightful." [Southern Lit. Messenger. 1475

SWORD AND DISTAFF. [by W: Gilmore Simms (1806-70): Charleston, Walker, 1852.] "In this work we recognize many of the characters of 'Katharine Walton' . . . Mr. Simms requires breathing room and space for action. In the stirring scenes of wild-wood life, the ambush, the surprise, the bush-fight, the camp-fire, and the break-nec hunt, he is pre-eminent. In his descriptions of the ruf-hewn and the half-polished specimens of bacwoods humanity, and in his rendering of their droll vernacular, he is perfect. His negroes ar living and breathing specimens of human ebony, and speaking with the very tongues of the genuine article." [Literary World. 1480

HORSE SHOE ROBINSON. [by J: P. Kennedy; 1831; Putnam, 1852.] "The time of the hero's adventures is the period of the 'Tory Ascendency' in the Carolinas, after the defeat of Gates, when the partisan leaders, Marion, Sumter, and Shelby, wer keeping up their guerilla warfare with Tarleton and Ferguson—of all in our history the era of romance. Horse Shoe is the ideal of the Whig partisan of those times. With a giant frame, great powers of endurance, frank, open-hearted, generous, bold, brave, quic-witted, full of expedients, a patriot true as steel, he takes irresistible hold of the affections of the readers of his adventures." [Norton's Lit. Gazette. 1485

THE SWAMP STEED. [N. Y., Dewitt, 1852.] "Marion and Jaspar, Moultrie and McDonald, English bullets and Charleston balls enliven its pages, and the roll of the drums, the clanging of trumpets, the charge of the squadron, the rattle of the muskets and crac of the rifle keep the reader wide awake from the first page to the last." [Literary World. 1490

CANOLLES [by J: Esten Cooke (1830-86): Detroit, Smith, 1877] "describes the fortunes of a freebooter, but brings in a number of historical characters, who seem generally life-like, and with no lac of incident. The hypercritical reader wil perhaps object to the frequency with which the sympathies ar racked by an impending execution at sunrise, but he wil hav to ascribe this frequency to the fortune of war, and there is enuf fiting and love-making to atone for whatever defects the book may hav. It is a good old-fashioned novel, without the subtleties of the modern novel, but telling its story with commendable distinctness and simplicity." [Nation. 1495

1781 Sept.

OLD HARBOR TOWN, The [by Augusta Campbell Watson: Dillingham, 1892.] "Is written unaffectedly and without the stilted tone into which historical novels ar apt to fall. Here and there a lapse of syntax betrays slight carelessness on the part of the author. The story is interesting, and is founded upon events which took place in those days at New London." [Boston "Literary World." 1497

1781 Oct.

YORKTOWN: Boston, Wells, 1827. 1505

1775-81.

THE REFUGEE. [by Matthew Murgatroyd, N. Y., 1825.] N. Y. 1500

SKETCH OF CONNECTICUT FORTY YEARS SINCE. [by Lydia (Huntley) Sigourney (1791-65): Hartford, 1824.] "The incidents ar neither few nor badly conceived, but they ar hung together so loosely and disjointedly that he must be a patriotic lover of Connecticut and its scenery,—of its rocky shores and proverbial habits, who can go resolutely throu the whole volume without misgiving or weariness... The episodes about Arnold and Champé want the indispensable requisite of novelty to giv them interest. There is value in the author's remarks on the now scattered tribe of Mohigans." [J. Sparks in N. Amer. Review. 1508

CHARLOTTE TEMPLE [by Susanna (Haswell) Rowson: 1790; N. Y., Lovell, 1888, Hurst, 1892] "written in the stilted, sentimental style of the day, still finds readers. In its main outlines it is a true story. The real name of Charlotte Temple was Charlotte Stanley, who was thrown on the streets of New York by her betrayer, Colonel Montresor, the Colonel Montraville of Mrs. Rowson's novel. Like the villain of the story, Colonel Montresor afterwards maried in New York. By a strange Nemesis his eldest son became engaged to his dauter by Charlotte Stanley. This part of the story is told in the sequel to 'Charlotte

Temple,' which was published after Mrs. Rowson's death under the title of 'Charlotte's Daughter.' " [Edinburgh Rev. 1510

CHARLOTTE'S DAUGHTER. [Boston, Richardson, 1828.] An admirable account by "Felix Oldboy" of the origin and growth of what he regards as the myth of Charlotte Temple was published in Frank Leslie's Monthly, Nov. 1890. 1511

FORSAKEN, THE: [1832.] "The events upon which this tale is founded ar supposed to hav taken place in Phil'a and its vicinity. The hero is Julian Hartfield, a lad of spirit, courage, ambition, learning, and two mistresses. It wer superfluous to say that these attributes, or at least the two latter, keep him constantly in trouble, until one of them is condemned, altho innocent, for the most unnatural crime a mother can commit, and by expiring beneath the gallows, leaves him at liberty to finish the story by a union with her rival. Among the other persons of the drama ar a hiwayman and his associates of both sexes,—criminals, drunkards, maniacs." [New England Mag. 1515

HAWKS OF HAWK-HOLLOW, The; a Tradition of Pennsylvania. [by Ro. M. Bird: Phil'a, Carey, 1835.] "In a little valley near the Delaware dwelt one Gilbert, an English emigrant. He had seven sons, all of whom displayed a spirit of desperate and recless adventure, and a love of the wild life of the woods and mountains... At the opening of the tale, a Captain Loring dwels upon the estate, and in the mansion of the Gilberts, holding them as the agent or tenant of a certain Col. Falconer, who is a second edition of Falkland in Caleb Williams, —and who has managed to possess himself of the property at Hawk-Hollo, upon its confiscation on account of the tory principles of the Hawks. During the happier days of the Gilberts, the life of this Falconer was preservd by three of them, upon a certain occasion of imminent peril... Grateful, however, for the kindness and evident affection of Jessie, and intoxicated with her beauty, he marries her in a moment of madness and passion—prevailing upon her to keep the marriage a secret for a short time. At this critical juncture, Falconer, who has already risen to honors and consideration in the world as an officer of the Colonial army, receives overtures of reconciliation both from his old patron and his dauter. His former flame is rekindled in his bosom. He puts off from day to day the publication of his marriage with Jessie, and finally, goaded by love and ambition, and encouraged by the accidental death of the regimental chaplain who married him, as wel as by that of the only witness to the ceremony, he flies from Jessie who is about to become a mother, and leaving herself and friends under the impression that the rite of marriage had been a mere mockery for the purpos of seduction, throes himself at once into the arms of his first love, and at length espouses her, a short time before the decease of Jessie, who dies in bringing a son into the world... Catherine Loring, however, is one of the sweetest creations ever emanating from the fancy of poet or of painter." [So. Lit. Messenger. 1520

EDGE HILL, by Ja. E. Heath, 1829. 1525

HERBERT WENDALL, Harper, 1835. 1530

LINWOODS, The. [by Catherine Maria Sedgwick (1789-1867): Harper, 1835.] "The scene is in New England and New York. We hav whigs and tories, soldiers and clowns, fine gentlemen and fine ladies, coxcombs and true men, most of whom play their parts 'excellently wel.' The hero, if a fine fello—combining all the sterling qualities of the New England character, with whose graces, accomplishment, and (as a hero ôt to hav) a dash of sentiment and romance, which ar not usually superadded to it, tho the union is by no means impossible." [New England Mag. 1535

MORTON'S HOPE. [by J: Lothrop Motley: 1839.] "The future historian, who spared no pains to be accurate, falls into the most extraordinary anachronisms in almost every chapter. Brutus in a bobwig, Othello in a swallo-tail coat, could hardly be more incongruously equipped than some of his characters in the manner of thôt, the phrases, the way of bearing themselvs which belong to them in the tale, but never could hav belonged to characters of our Revolutionary period. He goes so far in his carelessness as to mix dates in such a way as almost to convince us that he never looked over his own manuscript or proofs." [O. W. Holmes. 1540

ERNEST HARCOURT, or the Loyalist's Son. [Phil'a. Rockafellar, 1843.] Penn. 1545

BLACKPLUMED RIFLEMAN, The, by Newton M. Curtis: N. Y., Burgess, 1846. 1550

OLD CONTINENTAL, The, by J. K. Paulding: N. Y., Paine, 1846. 1555

PAUL ARDENHEIM, the Monk of Wissahikon [by G: Lippard: Peterson, 1849] "is a product of true creativ genius. We cannot say that its creations ar always to our taste, but they ar not the result of compilation, stil less of imitation. The story, tho professedly connected with a particular locality and with history, is yet purely imaginativ." [Sartain's Mag. 1560

WASHINGTON AND HIS GENERALS, or legends of the Revolution, by G: Lippard: new ed., Peterson, 1853. 1565

STANDISH, THE PURITAN [by "Eldred Grayson," i. e., J: Munson Bixby (1800-76): Harper, 1850] "opens with the parting of some collegians, one of whom joins the rebels, another the Tories, and the third goes into trade. The rebel falls in love with the sister of the Tory, and they two make up the poetry of the story. The trader contributes, as his share, to the humorous. And sundry historical personages, in nomenclature masquerade, ad to the excitement. The plot is not without interest. One or two of the characters ar managed with considerable dramatic skil. The style is not pretentious. The domestic scenes ar managed with the most effect; and the humorous scenes ar the most 'skippable.' We respect the author most hily for one thing; he has written a readable tale of the war without introducing us to Washington!" [Literary World. 1570

SCOUT, The, by B. Perley Poore: [new ed.] Boston, Studley, 1886. 1575

HARRY BURNHAM, or the Young Contluental, by H: S. Buckingham: N. Y., Burgess, 1851. 1580

CAMP-FIRES OF THE REVOLUTION; or the War of Independence illustrated by Thrilling Events and Stories by Continental Soldiers. [by H: C. Watson: Phil'a, Lindsay, 1851.] "The camp-fires of the Revolution, from Dorchester to Charleston and the Santee, ar presented in general description, when the soldiers of the encampment strike in with their vernacular to tel various stories." [Literary World.

HISTORY OF NORTH AMERICA.

THE MONARCHIST. [by J: B. Jones: Phil'a, Hart. 1853.] "Washington and other generals, American and British, flit rapidly across the scene. We see Gates, and Lee, and Conway, cabaling for power; Jefferson is shown at one moment penning prophecies of democracy, and in the next, fleeing at race-horse speed from the dragoons of Tarleton. The scene changes from Virginia to Philadelphia and other places. . . . The book shows reading and diligence on the part of the writer, who has scraped together a large body of interesting and curious revolutionary anecdote and illustration." [Southern Quarterly.]—One of the characters is Prince Charles Edward, who comes to America in the hope of inducing Washington to proclaim him king. 1585

SIMON KENTON, by J. Weir: Lippincott, 1853. 1590

OVERING. [by "Eldred Grayson": N. Y., Sheldon, 1854?] Rhode Island. 1595

AGNES, by M. H. Pike, Boston, Phillips, 1858. 1600

PERSONAL RECOLLECTIONS OF THE AMERICAN REVOLUTION [by L: Barclay: N. Y., Rudd, 1859] " professes to be a private journal, a domestic record of the occurrences of that important and eventful period. But the book, altho there may hav been some groundwork of contemporary memoranda in the form of journal or letters to base it upon, is plainly an imitation of the 'Diary of Lady Willoughby';—another imitation we should say, for the vein—not a very rich one at the best—has been much overworked. The author of this new 'diary' places his narrator on Long Island. The diary is full of exciting incidents and hairbreadth escapes in a small way." [Albion. 1605

EDWIN BROTHERTOFT. [by Th.

Winthrop: Ticknor, 1862.] "The scene is laid in New York. An ill-assorted marriage is the pivot of the plot. Evil results ensue. The husband, broken in spirit and blited in life, is separated from the coarse and guilty wife. Their dauter, groing up to womanhood, learns the mother's lesson of distrust and censure for the father. Presently that mother tries to force her into a marriage with a brutal personage. Circumstances reveal to her the true state of domestic affairs. Her father, who has joined the Colonial rebels, is informed of her peril, and, with several rebel friends, comes to her rescue. The interest of the story centers in this adventure. Its description occupies the greater part of the book. The effect is dramatic, tho marred by prolixity. The end is riteous and peaceful. As a whole the book leaves in the mind a scene of free, courageous, noble ideals, but no impression of either genius, art, or uncommon literary excellence." [Albion. 1610

BOYS AND GIRLS OF THE REVOLUTION, The [Lippincott. 1876] "consists of stories gathered from old journals, diaries and letters. Most of them ar, so far as we kno, new, and they ar certainly welcome. There is considerable inequality in the working up; all ar graphic and interesting, but some run overmuch into sentiment and what is called 'newspaper English,' such as 'glorious nobleness of this night's deeds.' Again, the term 'Boys and Girls' is made to include young men and women. These ar slight faults, however, and the book as a whole deserves to be popular. One of the best and truest to the title is 'The Little Black-eyed Rebel.'" [Nation. 1612

PETER AND POLLY. [by 'Marian

155

Douglas,' i. e., Annie Douglas (Green) Robinson (1842-); Boston, Osgood, 1876.] "Peter and Polly ar motherless twins, mere children at the outbreak of the war when the story opens, and when they ar sent by their father to an unknown aunt in New Hampshire, to whose care he entrusts them, himself at the same time joining the Continental army. Their long journey from Charlestown to her aunt's distant home, their somewhat loveless and unhappy life there, Peter's enlistment and departure for the army a few years later, and finally the close of the war, the return of the father and the reunion of the twins, ar told in a simple and attractiv manner. The story is as plain and unpretending as the times and manners of which it treats, and a story of this kind is as restful and as delightful as an hour spent among the furniture and furnishings of olden times, the spinnets and spinning wheels, the tall clocs, oaken cupboards, and rush-bottomed chairs of our grandmothers. In the opening chapter only, the style is labored, but all traces of this ar lost as the story progresses." [Library Table. 1615

GERALDINE HAWTHORNE, by B. M. Butt: Blackwood, 1883. 1620

GREAT TREASON, A. [by M. A. (Marks) Hoppus: Macmillan, 1883.] "Arnold is but an episode in a long history extending from the eve of the Boston Tea Party to the end of the war. For an historical novel, it is written with unusual grace and spirit, the fortunes of a young English officer and his sister forming the thread by which the various incidents ar bound. The book may wel be added to the short list of good illustrations of the Revolutionary War. Arnold is but one of many figures, tho the most thrilling pages of the book could not but be the capture and death of André." [Nation. 1625

GUERT TEN EYCK [by W: Osborn Stoddard: Lothrop, 1894] is "a tremendously exciting tale for boys. Almost all the action takes place in New York. Guert is a healthy, courageous boy, but he has some experiences which would turn a mature man's hair gray in a night, and he falls in with many notable people—Washington, Nathan Hale, Putnam, Burr, Monroe, Hamilton—some of them being at the time almost as young as he." [Godey's. 1630

As collateral reading:—

ROMANCE OF THE REVOLUTION, The. [by Oliver Bell Bunce: N. Y., Bunce, 1852.] "In a preliminary disquisition on the philosophy of history, the editor expresses the opinion that this volume, 'in being the legendary part of the history, will promote a better knoledge of the spirit of the time than can be derived from most any other source.'" [Norton's Lit. Gazette. 1635

LETTERS OF MRS. J: ADAMS [Boston, Little, 1840] "has hi claims to consideration: possessing a superior understanding, a noble spirit, and an excellent heart, she was, in all respects, one of the remarkable women of her day. These letters present her in her natural, unsophisticated character. We here see her just as she was, just as she thōt and acted at the different periods of her life, and in the different conditions throu which she passed. The letters written during the Revolutionary War and while her husband was on his first mission to Europe, present the most vivid pictures of those times of trial. Those from abroad, while she was with Mr. Adams on his second mission, abound in fresh and striking remarks upon the usages and manners of the hier ranks of society. Those written from New York, Philadelphia, and Washington, during the vice-presidency and presidency of her husband, ar filled with the most interesting details of the efforts of our infant nation to go alone, and interspersed with numerous curious reminiscences of the men and things of that day." [New York Review 1637

THE HUNDRED BOSTON ORATORS. [by Ja. Spear Loring: Boston, Jewett, 1852.] "It is pleasant to turn over Mr. Loring's gossiping pages. He writes con amore, to be sure, with a pen full of panegyric, which even patriotism wearies of in at the hundredth repetition; but we ar accustomed in such chronicles to a little vague enthusiasm, remembering that if there wer not a good deal of this commodity, no man could get throu the labors of celebrating so large a number of mixed notables and mediocrities. You cannot expect the critical powers of an Aristotle to be applied to such an undertaking. The man who puts his foot into such a thing wil not boggle at a puff. Delightful ar the unreservd communications of the genuin antiquarian. Facts ar facts in his eyes, and one pretty much of the same importance as another. Every date is an era. Every piece of prose broken into irregular lines is poetry. It is astonishing how much a certain species of tombstone verse enters into the New England chronicles. The poetic genius has produced no Spensers or Miltons in that region; but wel-ni every country schoolmaster and parish clergyman has paid the muse the compliment of recording his emotions in doggerel." [Literary World. 1640

WASHINGTON. [by Caroline Matilda (Stansbury) Kirkland (1801-64): Appleton, 1857.] "This work is intended especially for young readers; but many of every age wil enjoy it more than any other life of Washington. The only mark of its peculiar adaptation to the young is the omission of many 'details of battle and statesmanship, the cruelties of war and politics,' and the insertion in their stead of numerous personal anecdotes, not a few of which now first see the light. The writer has succeeded better than any other biographer in vivifying the image and memory of Washington, and had the book been written by a member of his own family, it could hardly hav furnished a more thoroly lifelike exhibition." [North Am. Review.]—A work having the same claims to attention as those mentioned above, but written by an author possessing a larger store of information, and better judgment in the choice of incidents to be described, is the Life of Washington by H. E. Scudder, Houghton, 1890. 1645

THROUGH COLONIAL DOORWAYS. [by A., Hollingsworth Wharton: Lippincott, 1893.] "Old Philadelphia is so full of colonial and revolutionary memories that a peep throu its doorways into its comfortable 'old timey' interiors is a lesson in American history. Miss Wharton knows much about these graceful colonial trifles,—folk-lore and quaint tales of old Philadelphia society, when Lord Howe and Major André wer prominent figures in it, and famous tea-drinkings, when the meschianza was at its hight. She opens an old lavender-scented chest and lets out a whif of delightful things; old faces in antique frames become young again; tie-wigs encircle rosy faces, and beauty-spots glisten on complexions already too dazzling. Her chapters revive the faded recollections of the Sally Wisters, Eliza Southgates, and Abigail Adamses of other days—colonial 'grandes dames' who figure in the floral and florid memories of the time. Naturally, Dr. Franklin, in pumps and periwig, comes in often; faded Jersey beauties and Baltimore belles rejoice in temporary rejuvenation; yello love-letters open and reveal the 'broken hearts' and Johnsonian hyperbole of 1784, and quotations from The Gentleman's Magazine appropriately epitaph the heavily-slumbering, half-awakened courtships and marriages of old Philadelphia families of the era of Valley Forge. Many of these families wer stanchly Tory, and 'stuc to their ease and Madeira' when Yankee rebels wer watching for the whites of their enemies' eyes not far from Bunker Hill. The receptions and assemblies, the minuets and card-parties, the dabblings in philosophy and science of this imitativ period ar faithfully described from original documents and shed agreeable light on hier and more complicated subjects." [Nation. 1650

SOCIAL LIFE IN OLD NEW ENGLAND. [by Alice Morse Earle: Scribner, 1894.] "The author's style is delightful, and almost every page is interesting. She devotes this volume to the social side of the Puritan's life, treating child-life, courtship and marriage, domestic service, home interiors, table plenishings. We ride with her on turnpikes and understand the ways of travel and the mysteries of the tavern. With bright colors she shos that the inborn love of the Teutonic races for holidays and festivals could not be repressed even by Judaistic Puritanism. 'Raiment and Vesture' ar displayed before us, and doctors and patients wel described... To sho her willingness to face the facts usually ignored by glorifiers of the Yankee Puritans, the author devotes one or two pages to the New England custom of 'bundling,' but does not seem to kno how widely prevalent it was. Almost as a matter of course she refers it to the nauty nēbors of the Yankees, evidently not thinking it possible that it should hav come from England, tho in reality it had been notoriously prevalent for centuries on all the coasts of northwestern Europe." [Critic. 1655

1781-1812

THE PRAIRIE. [by Ja. Fenimore Cooper: Phil'a, Carey, 1827.] "The action of the piece is religiously confined to the prairie. The events of the story happen to a bee-hunter and his sweetheart, and a captain in the army and his wife. The troubles in which both these couples ar involved ar occasioned partly by a family of squatters, consisting of a termagant woman, her gigantic husband and knavish brother, and a troop of overgrown girls and boys; and partly by a tribe of cruel and thievish Indians, the Sioux, Tetons, or Dahcotahs, for the author calls them indiscriminately by either of these names. On the other hand, these good people hav for their friends and helpers in calamity, a stupid, pedantic naturalist, a sagacious trapper, and a magnanimous and friendly tribe of Indians, the Pawnee Loups. The unlawful detention of the Captain's wife in the squatter family, and her final restoration to her husband, the opposition of this family to the marriage of the bee-hunter with his sweetheart, their relativ; these incidents, diversified with a brief captivity among the Sioux, and a battle between this tribe and the Pawnees, form the thread of the story. This it not very promising matter, but it is handled by a man of genius, and wrôt up, we should think, into all the interest of which it is capable. The author's power of narration and description does not desert him;—the faculty of setting before the mind of the reader, with a strong distinctness, a kind of visibility, the personages of the story and their actions,— a faculty of immense importance to the writer of fictitious narrativ, and one on the possession of which a great deal of the popularity of Mr. Cooper is founded.., With Leatherstocking, altho now introduced for the third time, we profess ourselvs hily pleased. This personage is one of Mr. Cooper's happiest creations, and one upon which he must mainly depend for his future fame. The character of this philosopher of the woods, who had engrafted upon a Christian stoc many of the wild virtues of savage life, is represented as touched but not changed by the decline of life. He has retired, it is true, from the forest to the prairie, before the settlements which gain so fast upon the wilderness, and has been obliged by his change of abode and the infirmity of his stage of life, to change his vocation of hunter to that of trapper; but we find in him the same sagacity, the same adoption of Indian prejudices, and the same continual reference to the maxims of wisdom supplied by the experience of uncivilized life, the same kindness of heart, and something of the same warmth of imagination. All these qualities ar, however, beautifully tempered by an additional infusion of that caution and forbearance with which old age naturally seeks to protect its increasing infirmity." [U. S. Lit. Gazette. 1655

TOKEAH, or the White Rose [by " C: Sealsfield." i. e., C: Postl: Phil'a, Carey, 1829] "is in the same walk with Cooper's novels, and wil bêar comparison with them. With less originality and power in single characters and scenes, there is more sustained and uniform beauty throughout, and in the delineation of female character a skil to which Mr. Cooper has not approachd. We do not kno of two more beautiful creations than Canondah and Rosa. The latter especially, a Spanish captiv reared in the hut of the chief Miko of the Occonees, is drawn with exquisit tenderness. The descriptions ar evidently the work of a man who has been accustomed to observ, and who has looked on nature with the eye of a poet. It is altogether a most delightful book, and a credit to our literature." [Amer. Monthly Mag. 1660

WESTERN CAPTIVE, The, or the Times of Tecumseh: by E.. Oakes Smith: N. Y., Winchester, 1842. 1665

YOUNG, or the Rescue: a tale of the Great Kanawha: Harper, 1844. 1670

TALES OF THE NORTHWEST [by W: J. Snelling (†1848): Boston(?), 1837] "is the most faithful picture of Indian life ever written." Catlin, quoted in Lit. World. 1675

As collateral reading:—
MEN OF THE BACKWOODS, The. [by "Ascott Ro. Hope," i. e., A. Ro. H. Moncrieff: N. Y., Dutton, 1880.] "Most of the good stories of early bacwoods life ar collected in this volume and retold in an entertaining manner. The book may be read with interest by any one who loves stories of adventures in the wilderness. The author has divided the volume into two parts, the first of which is devoted to the white men, the second to the Redskins; and without observing an exact historical

order, he has so arranged his sketches as to trace throu the half century during which a constant struggle was going on with the western savages, the principal events which characterized it from the first appearance of the settlers in the valley of Ohio, to the fall of Tecumseh. The concluding chapters giv a great deal of valuable information about the redman's religion, manners, and ordinary way of life, which has apparently been derived from books of authority." [Nation. 1680

SOUTHWEST [by Jo. Holt Ingraham (1809-60): Harper, 1836] " is a clever and agreeable work. It seems the transcript of an acute, observing, and wel-cultivated mind, and is enriched with much fanciful and gloing description." [Amer. Mon. Mag. 1685

RICHARD HURDIS. [by W: Gilmore Simms: 1837, new ed., N. Y., 1855.] " The reader is introduced to scenes and characters peculiar to the ruffest border life. Robbery and murder, and the dark and lawless passions whence they spring, ar the ordinary excitements by which the interest is provoked and sustained. If the subject wer as pleasing as the execution is able, we might congratulate Mr. Simms on his success, but we must confess our delight when we at last escaped from the company into which he had tempted us by his skil." [Graham's Mag. 1690

WESTWARD HO. [by Ja. Kirke Paulding: Harper, 1832.] " The characters ar original and wel drawn. The Virginia planter who squanders his estates in a prodigal hospitality, and with the remnants of a liberal fortune seeks a new home in the untried forests; Zeno and Judith Paddock, a pair of village inquisitors; and Bushfield, an untamed western hunter, ar all actual and indigenous beings. Mr. Paulding had already sketched the Kentuckian, with a freer but less skilful hand, in his comedy of Nimrod Wildfire. Whoever wanders in the footsteps of Daniel Boone wil still meet with Bushfields, tho until he approaches nearer the Rocky Mountains the ruf edges of the character may be somewhat softened; and Dangerfields ar not yet strangers in Virginia." [Griswold's Prose Writers, 1846. 1695

—— SAME (" The Banks of the Ohio "). London, 1833. 1696

GEORGE BALCOMB. [by Nathaniel Beverley Tucker (1784-1851): N. Y., Harper, 1836.] " As a spirited and interesting picture of Western life and people, it is the most correct we hav ever read." [Ladies' Companion. 1700

NICK OF THE WOODS [by Ro. M. Bird: Phil'a(?), 1837] " is a 'raw-head and bloody bones' story. A tale of veritable horrors, whose incidents prove that there are other griefs in life besides those which spring from a condition of things which makes one glad to borro money at fifty per cent. Dr. Bird has at length planted his foot on the real soil of romance—' the dark and bloody ground' of Kentucky, the little district where the first children of what is now a great state wer literally cradled in fire—doing, daring, and suffering more than did ever band of colonists upon any shore. . . The present wild tale is, in all its scenes and characters, thoroly and completely American. The horrors and extravagancies it commemorates wil be viewed with emotion akin to disgust by some criticks [sic] who, ignorant of the singular fidelity of the descriptions, wil regard them as a prurient catering for the morbid taste of the day. To others, however, they wil breathe the very spirit of historical truth." [N. Y. Mirror.

—— SAME, ed. W: H. Ainsworth, 1843. "Cooper's redmen, with their apocryphal virtues, ar a class by themselvs. Dr. Bird disputes all the good qualities with which Cooper has invested these savages. In the Last of the Mohicans—the most vigorous portion of that series of volumes which biographize the hunter of the wood in the various stages of life—Cooper has endowed these scalping wanderers with the noblest attributes of educated minds—I mean the temperance, self-mastery, and sense of justice, to the inculcation of which education is usually considered necessary. Bird takes precisely the opposit line, and writes down the unfortunate redskins with all the hatred which a civilized colonist may be supposed to entertain for them. It is very unimportant which of the novelists is right; in all probability the truth is to be found in the fact that Cooper sketched the free, and Bird the corrupted tribe; but in strength of drawing—and therefore apparent likelihood—Cooper's Indian sketches ar far superior to those of his antagonist." [Albion. 1705

BEAUCHAMPE. [by W: Gilmore Simms: Phil'a, Lea, 1842.] Kentucky. 1710

LONZ POWERS; or The Regulators [by James Weir: Lippincott, 1850] "describes Kentucky life as it was when the border contests of savages and squatters had just ceased, but the settled ordinances of civil life had not been established; when, among those disappearing 'forests primeval' was scattered a rude, unlettered, but hardy race of pioneers, interspersed with organized bands of desperadoes of the very worst description. Mr. Weir, we presume, is a nativ Kentuckian. At all events, he appears to be familiar with all the local traditions of the state, and he has made a book of much value, as wel for its historical reminiscences as its exciting scenes of adventure." [Sartain's Mag. 1715

As collateral reading:—

DANIEL BOONE, AND THE HUNTERS OF KENTUCKY. [by W: H: Bogart (1810-): new ed., N. Y., Miller, 1856.] Boone is here described "not merely as the reckless adventurer and pioneer, but as a patriot and sage. He certainly displayed the gentler, no less than the hardier, traits of the true hero; and his virtues would hav made him the ornament of civilized society, had not his exposures and privations laurd him to rudeness of a border life, and made its wild sports, ruf encounters, and thic-sown perils a necessity of his nature. . . To the life of Boone is added an interesting series of biographies of the early hero-hunters of Kentucky." [North Am. Review. 1720

OLD HICKS THE GUIDE, or Adventures in the Camanche Country in search of a Gold Mine. [by C. W. Webber: Harper, 1848.] "This is a racy and startling book; full of the wild and wonderful; presenting such a rapid succession of stirring incidents that we scarcely remember a work in this respect its superior. The author does not study so much to tel his story in a polished diction, as he does to convey vivid pictures of border life adventure; his readers, however, wil be unanimous in regarding this as a decided advantage. We hav not time nor space to refer to the several characters who figure in these pages, but must content ourselves with simply commending the work to the perusal of all who wish for a stirring narrativ of adventure among the semi-civilized inhabitants of the southwestern border [Texas]." [Albion.]

—" It is curious as a picture of Indian adventures, and the romantic character of some of the personages of the story. It is a rapid, lively, readable narrativ, in which the reader, however, is carried rather about than forward, the Gold Mine being as out of the way at the end as at the beginning of the story. The whole is, however, understood to be based upon tradition and legend." [Literary World.]—A sequel to above, called "The Goldmines of the Gila," was published by Dewitt in 1849. 1725

MAY MARTIN [by Daniel Pierce Thompson: new ed., Boston: Mussey, 1852] "is a tale suggested by the operations of a band of adventurers who engaged in searching for hidden treasure among the Green Mountains." [Norton's. 1730

ADRIAN, or the Clouds of the Mind. [by G: P. R. James and B. Field: London, Boone, 1852.] "The scene is in America soon after the war, and the feelings or rather prejudices meant to be illustrated by the narrativ ar such as a collision between the old growth of English monarchical opinions and the new graft of American republican notions might be expected to elicit. The 'deus ex machinâ' is not very new or successful, however; and we cannot think it the right way to conquer a prejudice against lo birth that we should hav to admit the birth after all to be by no means so lo as we thôt it. Nevertheless there is pleasing writing in the story, several sound reflections, and some vivid local painting." [Examiner. 1735

MARRYING BY LOT. [by C. B. Mortimer: Putnam, 1868.] Moravians in Penn. 1740

A VICTORIOUS DEFEAT. [by Wolcott Balestier: Harper, 1886.] "The 'Judæa' of the story is obviously Bethlehem in Pennsylvania. The story attempts a picture of the colony as it appeared to the eyes of a young Englishman coming thither shortly after the Revolution. He falls in love with the doctor's beautiful dauter, thus bringing himself into rivalry with the pastor of the congregation. There ar practically but two incidents in the whole story— the public reproof of the heroin, Constance Van Cleef, before the congregation, for her suspected partiality for the English stranger, as one outside the Moravian communion; and the appeal to 'the lot' to decide the question of the marriage of Constance and the minister. So far as motivs and convictions ar involved, it all belongs as completely to a vanished world as the scenes of the 'Scarlet Letter,' and only such a hand as Hawthorne's could make it liv again." [Nation. 1745

A LOYAL LITTLE RED-COAT. [by Ruth Ogden: N. Y., Stokes, 1890.] "The heroin is a stanch adherent of the King, altho the war is over. But Hazel's father had, with great personal loss, folloed his convictions, and Hazel loyally folloed him. Her intervue with Hamilton, and the fearlessness and naive simplicity with which she givs her opinions on a case which the great lawyer had defended, is one of the best chapters. The Van Vleet tea-party has a genuin colonial flavor." [Nation. 1750

1782.

JOURNAL OF A YOUNG LADY IN VIRGINIA. [Baltimore, Murphy, 1871.] "This young lady of Virginia wrote her journal, which covers only a part of the year 1782, in the form of letters. Indeed, it does not happen that she was in the habit of keeping a journal when she was at home, and apparently we owe the pleasant little record here published to the fact that in the fall of 1782 she went to the since famous Wilderness to make a round of visits among her relativs, the Washingtons, Lees, Gordons, etc. Her surname is not known, and her friend was Polly Brent, so the diary, folloing the fashion of those days, is 'from Lucinda to Marcia.' It is very entertaining, with its flavor of old times and with its shadoings of our dead-and-gone-great-great-grandmothers when they wer girls. Altho written in the fall of 1782, there is no indication that, less than a year before, a relativ of our young lady of Virginia had compelled the surrender of Cornwallis at Yorktown. It is interesting, too, for it hints as to the manners of the Old Dominion in those days; and the young lady herself, 'Lucinda,' is a very taking figure." [Nation. 1755

1786.

THE INSURGENTS. [by Ralph Ingersoll Lockwood: Phil'a, 1835.] Shay's rebellion. 1760

1787.

MODERN CHIVALRY. [by Hugh H: Brackenridge: Phil'a, Carey, 1847.] "The adventures of Capt. Farrago and Teague O'Regan wer first published some 50 years ago in a village west of the Alleghany Mts., at the close of the whiskey insurrection, to scenes and occurrences in connexion with which many of its pages ar given. The captain of course is the representativ of Don Quixotte, a clear-headed man, whose independent way of looking at things from living out of the world, has gained him the credit of eccentricity. He is withal a practical wag, setting out with his Irish servant in search of adventures.

The gist of his observations and experiences lies in this, that the duties and responsibilities of a new state of society hav been thrust upon a new race of men so suddenly, that, unused to their new democratic privileges, they ar very much in the way of abusing them. Without political knoledge they send the weaver to Congress; without learning they get up a philosophical society for leatherheads, and appoint, after the fashion of Dr. O'Toole, a nativ Irishman to a Greek professorship." [Literary World. 1765

1795-1800.

MILES WALLINGFORD: Sequel to Afloat and Ashore. [by Ja. Fenimore Cooper: N. Y., 1844.] "The aim of the work is to illustrate the hazards run and the wrongs suffered by neutral vessels in the mity struggle between England and Bonaparte. Hence the chief action of the story is at sea; and never has there been a more just or a more spirited picture of the skil, daring and perilous adventures of sailors than appears in this narrativ of the voyage of the 'Dawn.' Falling into the hands of one belligerent after the other only to rise upon the prize crews and regain their command. the leading characters had an opportunity to see how British and French handled and fôt their frigates, and also to sho them how difficult it was to hold an American merchantman, tho the seizure might eventually destroy the property, and thus cripple for a time the irrepressible energies of a restless and rising nation. In fine, it is a great historical painting. In no one of his tales of the ocean has Mr. Cooper displayed more inventiv faćulty, given more scenic effect, or created a more powerful cast of character." [Home Journal. 1770

THE STORY OF KENNETT. [by Bayard Taylor: N. Y., Hurd, 1866.] Pennsylvania.—See No. 958. 1775

PHILIP NOLAN'S FRIENDS. [by E: Everett Hale (1822-): Scribner, 1877.] "The scene is partly in Louisiana, in the then Franco-Spanish town of Orleans, partly in the region lying between the Mississippi and San Antonio. Louisiana was under Spanish rule, tho on the point of being ceded to France [1800]. It was a time of great uncertainty and misrule. The Spanish officials wer jealous of each other's power and of Yankees and Kentuckians. Philip Nolan was one of the latter, a pioneer skilled in woodcraft and in the customs and speech of the wild tribes inhabiting the wilderness. Armed with a Spanish passport, he and a handful of followers start westward from Natchitoches to capture wild horses for the use of the Spaniards. But the authorities on the further side of the river persist in considering Nolan the general of a filibustering expedition, and finally kill him. Against this historical bacground is woven the romance of 'Philip Nolan's Friends.' Two ladies ar sent from Orleans to San Antonio in Nolan's care. Of course they meet with many adventures, and vivid descriptions ar given of their camp-life, their meetings with Redmen, and of life at the Spanish military posts. Many characters ar introduced of various nationalities, but all ar original and wel drawn. The book is written in Mr. Hale's peculiar and, to our thinking, rather disjointed style, but it is bright and exceedingly interesting." [Library Table.] —According to Boston Pub. Ly. Cat., the time is that of Burr's conspiracy [1806]. 1780

DERWENT [by "J: Chester," i. e., J: Mitchell (-1870): N. Y., Randolph, 1872] "consists of reminiscences which extend into the last century, and treat the rudeness and natural pleasures of country living in the days when coal and lucifer matches wer as yet unknown, the whipping-post still in use, the Puritan Sabbath reckoned from sundown of Saturday to sundown of Sunday... This picture, with the reflections and observations which accompany it, of New England ways in the 'good old times,' especially commends itself to grown readers, who wil find its descriptions faithfully drawn and the sentiment noticeably pure and true, lapsing neither into affectation nor into commonplace. The author's style wil also gratify the same class, shoing as it does the marks of civilization and of self-restraint, and being withal so simple as to make it possible for large extracts to be read aloud with but little alteration to the youngest audience. A child of 3, not less than one of 10 or 15, can listen eagerly to the story of fetching fire, going to mil, fetching cows, of jac-o'-lanterns, sheep, dogs, and birds." [Nation. 1785

IN OLD QUINNEBASSET. [by "Sophie May," i. e. Rebecca Sophia Clarke: Boston, Lee, 1891.] "A more graceful and charming tale it would be hard to find. Here is old Quinnebasset with its associations and memories, its old houses and fireplaces, and here ar the very people walking its streets, discussing the electoral votes in the same formal English as during Washington's time. And here is the heroin keeping a diarum, which she fils with quaint girlish fancies, and doing all the old-fashioned household tasks—spinning, making possets, discoursing on religion, getting into mischief, dressing for a grand ball, teasing her suitors, and being as bewitching and merry as Miss Clarke's heroins always ar, and as full of spontaneous life as the original from whom we suspect this same Elizabeth Gilman was drawn." [Critic. 1790

As collateral reading:—

RECOLLECTIONS OF S: BRECK. with passages from his Note-books (1771-1862). [Edited by H. E. Scudder: London, Low, 1878.] "Breck was the son of a wealthy merchant in Boston, who sent him to school in France. He mixed in the best American society, and was privileged to see many distinguished strangers... Mr. Breck's anecdotes of Boston society at the end of the last century are very entertaining, and form by far the best part of his book. Out of his most amusing reminiscences is an account of Mrs. Jeffrey, a sister of J: Wilkes, who seems to hav had hardly less eccentric force than her brother." [Examiner. 1795

1804 Feb.

DECATUR AND SOMERS [by Molly Elliot Seawell: Appletons, 1894] "is a pleasant story, narrating two of the most touching and heroic passages in the history of our navy, the destruction of the Philadelphia off Tripoli, and the explosion of the Intrepid. The author has not, however, told it in a better way than Maclay tels it in his history, and has not, we think, equaled in pathos or interest her own story of 'Little Jarvis.' Her picture of naval life contains many errors and anachronisms. Historically the incidents ar true, tho the traditions of the service ar that Stewart, Decatur [1779-1820], and Somers wer intimate alike with each other, and that the Intrepid grounded before she was blown up Miss Seawell will not hav written in vain, however, if she make known exploits of the American navy one of which was characterized by Nelson as 'the most bold and daring act of the age.'" [Nation. 1800

1804 July.

RIVALS, The. [by Jere. Clemens (1814-65): Lippincott, 1860.] "The author has successfully defended the memory of Burr from the calumnies which hav been heaped upon it. Burr had faults which all regret, but he also had great abilities, which entitle his name to receive an honorable recognition from his countrymen. Of the great men of the early history of the republic, none wer possessed of nobler traits and actuated by more generous impulses." [Home Journal.]—The author was senator 1849-53. 1805

1806.

A VICTIM OF INTRIGUE. [by Ja. W. Taylor: Peterson, 1847.] Burr. 1810

THE TRAITOR. [by Emerson Bennett: Cin'ti, Stratton, 1850.] Burr. 1815

THE CONSPIRATOR. [by Eliza A. Dupuy: Appleton, 1850.] "The extraordinary adventures of that extraordinary man, Aaron Burr, form the groundwork of the tale; and interwoven with them ar love-passages, incidents, local descriptions, and dramatic scenes, many and varied—the whole servd with considerable freshness, tho occasionally marred by a too obvious attempt at fine writing. The tale opens at Blennerhasset's Island." [Albion. 1820

THE CONSPIRACY OF BURR, N. Y., Simmons, 1854. 1825

THE MAN WITHOUT A COUNTRY, by E: E, Hale: Boston, 1864. 1830

ZACHARY PHIPPS [by Edwin Lassetter Bynner (1842-92): Houghton, 1892] "is a tale of the good old times. We hope those times wer really good enuf to condone the badness of a boy who ran away to sea at the tender age of 8, and to permit him, when barely of age, to become an acceptable Legation's attaché in London. Certainly Zachary did far better than if he had been good and stayed at home and pursued humdrum knoledge under the shado of Master Tilleston's cane. Whatever of national importance was going on from Boston to Florida, he managed to be in it. A most innocent accomplice of treason, he made one of the picturesque Washita expedition planned in the angry heart of Burr. Barely old enuf to blo a whistle, he shared the Constitution's naval fame. Again, in the hand-to-hand tussle between the Chesapeake and Shannon, he was literally right on dec. As a climax of adventure, to him was it given to witness those atrocities in Florida which make Jackson appear more of a murderer than a soldier. Zachary's career makes a capital book for youthful readers, and is not without serious interest. The author's historical vision, while patriotic, is unprejudiced, and he givs history a dramatic value without distortion of facts. Some touches of characterization ar very vivid—for instance, in the passing glimpses of Mrs. Blennerhasset and of Burr. Burr's last appearance in New York, poor and persistently dishonest, apparently unmoved by private neglect and public scorn, yet sorro-stricken by the death of his grandchild, makes one feel, not how ignoble he was, but how noble he might hav been." [Nation. 1845

An illustrated article on the Blennerhasset house may be found in Emerson Bennett's Mag., vol. I., p. 408.

1808.
SCENES AT WASHINGTON [Harper, 1848] "is a wel told story; but it derives its chief interest from the fact that it has all the appearance of a painting from life. Besides hitting off with good effect many of the usages of the time, it givs a good idea of some prominent characters, and hints at some important events in the political history of the country. It would seem to hav been written by some one old enuf to draw from his memory reminiscences of things which occurred half a century ago." [Am. Lit. Mag.]—" The scenes described ar obviously drawn from authentic sources; or as far as they ar imaginary, founded on the recognized opinions and manners of the period. Such characters as Gouverneur Morris and J: Randolph ar graphically described." [Literary World. 1840

LAFITTE: THE PIRATE OF THE GULF. [by Jo. Holt Ingraham: Harper, 1836.] "An expatriated Frenchman dwels upon the banks of the Kennebec. He has two sons. . . The lovers meet by moonlight, and ar overheard by the discarded brother, who in a moment of frenzy plunges a knife in the bosom of Henri, hurries to the sea-coast, and, seizing the boat of a fisherman, pushes out immediately to sea. Upon the eve of being lost he is picked up by a merchant vessel, and proceeds on a voyage to the Mediterranean. The vessel is captured by the Algerines—our hero is imprisoned—escapes by the aid of a Moorish maiden, whom he dishonors and abandons—is recaptured—escapes again in an open boat for Ceuta—is again captured by Algerines—unites with them, and subsequently commands them—is taken by the Turks—is promoted in their navy—turns Mussulman—becomes the chief of an armed horde—combats in the Egyptian ranks—becomes again a pirate—is taken by the Spaniards—is liberated and becomes a corsair again and again. Its adventures so far, however, ar related in language little more diffuse than ours." [So. Lit. Messenger. 1845

As collateral reading:—

The REAL LAFITTE, a series of articles, by Ja. Rees, in The New World, 1841. 1850

The CREOLE. [by Jo. B. Cobb.] New Orleans. 1855

LEGENDS OF THE WEST. [by James Hall: Phil'a, Hall, 1832.] "The legends ar fictitious, but ar founded on incidents which hav been witnessed by Mr. Hall, or upon traditions preservd by the people. Mr. Hall has a fine tact in describing the border warfare, the rifle-shooting, the solemn scenery of the thic woods, the lingering love of the emigrant for the 'old States,' the evening-fires of the camp-meeting, and the whole range of Western men and manners." [Amer. Quarterly Observer. 1860

THE BANDITS OF THE OSAGE. [by Emerson Bennett; Cin'ti, Robinson.] Ohio. 1865

GOMERY OF MONTGOMERY, N. Y., Carleton, 1865. 1870

As collateral reading:—

PIONEER WOMEN OF THE WEST. [by E. Fries (Lummis) Ellet: Scribner, 1852.] "The annals of western emigration abound in instances of every species of heroism. The hardships and perils which belong to pioneer life, especially as it presented itself to those who first crossed the Mississippi, ar scarcely surpassed by any which wer encountered by the early occupants of the Atlantic coast. Among both classes of settlers it was often the case that women wer called upon to make sacrifices and endure trials which tasked the sternest fortitude and the loftiest heroism of her nature. To gather some of these instances and bring them forth from the obscurity in which they hav been buried, is the design of Mrs. Ellet in this pleasant volume. It is a work which, from the fleeting character of its materials, must be accomplished, if ever, while the incidents and characters which it records ar fresh in the recollections of men; and we ar glad to find it undertaken by a lady who has already done so much to illustrate those heroins of humble life who adorned the Revolutionary period." [Christian Review. 1875

1810-21.

COSTAL. [by Gabriel Ferry: J. Blackwood, 1857.] Mexico. 1880

1812-14.

ELKSWATAWA, THE PROPHET OF THE WEST [by Ja. S. French: Harper, 1836] "is wel worth reading for the sake of becoming acquainted with a single character, Earthquake, the Kentucky hunter. The story, too, altho the plot is simple, is so wel managed as to keep a lively interest. And here our praise must end, unless, indeed, we pause to thank the author for having used his efforts in freshening the history of a man whose name ôt never to be forgotten while heroism and love of country ar deemed worthy of being remembered, Tecumseh." [Amer. Monthly Mag. 1885

EONEGUSKI. [Washington, 1839.] "The action begins with the description of the family of Robert Aymor, one of the pioneers of the wilds. His dauter Atha is loved by J: Welsh, a half-breed, saved when a child by one of Aymor's nebors during one of the earlier skirmishes with the Redmen. Her father wil not consent to their union oing to the savage blood in his veins, and his love drives him from that part of the country—he becomes the adopted son of an old chief. . . A story such as this affords many opportunities for fine descriptiv and narrativ writing, of which the author, indeed, has not failed to avail himself, in proof of which we might instance the intervue between Tecumseh, who has been introduced with signal effect, and Eoneguski, and the battle where Gen. Jackson drowned in blood the last remnant of the hostil Redmen." [Democratic Review.]—Scene: N. C. 1890

As collateral reading:—

RED EAGLE [by G: Cary Eggleston: Dodd, 1878] "is the only book devoted exclusivly to the history of the Creek war, and to the character and achievements of Red Eagle, alias W: Weatherford. The work has very properly rescued from oblivion the name and fame of an aboriginal military genius. Details about Tecumseh, Pushmatahaw, and Generals Jackson, Claiborne, Coffee and other actors in an important struggle, as wel as of the operations of the British and Spanish allies of the insurgent Indians, ar also collated from numerous sources, to the general advantage of historic truth. It is, however, to be regretted that the literary execution wil not render the volume attractive to the public. The romantic incidents of the war wer quite equal to those of the siege of Detroit, but we miss the vivid descriptions by which Parkman gave to his 'History of the Conspiracy of Pontiac' such absorbing interest." [Nation. 1885

LIFE AMONGST THE INDIANS. [by G: Catlin (1796-1872): Appleton, 1867.] "Any father of a family who is willing that his boys should read Cooper's novels or Mayne Reid's, and would prefer to hav them avoid dime novels and the unnatural backwoods romances of Dr. J. H. Robinson or Emerson Bennett, wil do wel to get this. . . The author is himself a hily interesting character, and he not only writes in an exceptionally good style, but with sense as rare and humanity by no means common. His words breathe only sincerity and truthfulness, even where—as when he acquits the Redmen of having ever been cannibals—he speaks too sweepingly in favor of a much-slandered race. Both volumes ar divided between North and South America, and in an unexaggerated narrativ of actual adventure the boy-reader is most agreeably transported over plains and down rivers and along foreign coasts, learning nothing but what he wil be the better for remembering, and getting a much better idea of the Redmen than one adult in a thousand has. If we wer teaching school we should make this book and 'Last Rambles amongst the Indians of the Rocky Mountains and the Andes,' a text-book of American history and geography—such a text-book, let us ad, as under slavery could never hav been tolerated in this country. For when, prior to 1860, would a school committee hav approved chapter IX. of the 'Life,' which tels the shameful truth about the Georgia and Florida Redmen?" [Nation. 1900

CASIMIR SARAL, by Bernard A. Reynolds: Charleston, 1830(?). 1905

THE CANADIAN BROTHERS. [by J: Richardson: Montreal, Armour, 1840.] "This graphic work is the sequel to 'Wacousta, or the Prophecy.' But the book has qualities of a more important nature than those of a pleasing work of fiction; it is a picture of the state of

affairs in the provinces, 1812-15." [Albion. 1915
—— SAME ("Matilda Montgomerie"). Dewitt, 1851. 1916
KABAOSA, or The Warriors of the West. [by Anna L. Snelling: Boston, 1842.] 1920
WAUNANGEE, or the Massacre at Chicago; N. Y., Long, 1852. 1925
CRUISING IN THE LAST WAR, by C: J. Peterson: Peterson, 1850. 1930
THE MISSING BRIDE, or Miriam the Avenger. [by E. D. E. (N.) Southworth: Peterson, 1855.] "The incidents, as the reader may judge from the terrific title, ar of the intensest sort of 'thrilling' interest. The admirers of Mrs. Southworth, and she has created many by her passionately sensuous style, wil no doubt find this work hily entertaining. For us, we never sup on horrors with any satisfaction, nor can we approve that class of fiction to which the previous works of this lady belong." [So. Lit. Messenger. 1935
WITHIN THE CAPES. [by Howard Pyle: London, Warne, 1885.] "The capes between whose points the tale opens and closes ar those of Chesapeake Bay. What givs a most pleasant flavor to the book and makes it of genuin literary importance, despite its unpretending modesty, is the skill with which the author transports us in the midst of a simple and pastoral people, and makes us see and understand their ways and manners. He presents to us a Quaker settlement where people and place ar alike charming; the men ar grave and brave; the women ar gentle and beautiful; there is a rolling landscape and a fertil soil. . . Here is variety enuf, and it is set before us skilfully, with a certain old-fashioned quaintness of a pleasant flavor." [Saturday Review. 1940

MIDSHIPMAN PAULDING. [by Mollie Elliot Seawell: Appleton, 1891.] "The story of young Paulding's adventure with the Dutch landlord and of the winter at Sackett's Harbor is told with considerable snap. . . The way he acted when under fire, and the way the brilliant victory of McDonough on Lake Champlain was fôt, and what part Midshipman Paulding took in it—all this is wel told. The book stics to facts without being matter-of-fact or prosy in style." [Critic. 1945

1815-20.

GREY HAWK. [by J: Tanner: Lippincott, 1883.] "An unadorned tale of life on the Red River of the North in the early part of this century is the autobiografical history of J: Tanner's captivity. This, edited by Edwin James, the historian of Long's expedition to the Rocky Mountains, was a classic, in its way, more than 50 years ago. It has now been condensed and reprinted under English editorship, as 'Grey Hawk.' It is the true story of a little boy, stolen in Kentucky by Shawnees, who grew up adopted and naturalized among the Ottawas, to whom he was transferred by purchase. Its interest lies in its direct speech and in its homely details of the barbarism and poverty of nomadic hunters, often distressed for want of food and often in misery from rum. The savage virtue of hospitality and the civilized vice of drunkenness have many examples in its pages, and one learns that life among the less fierce tribes of the Northwest was an irregular succession of hunting, starvation, very translent abundance and carousing, cold, and poverty." [Nation. 1950
SNOW-SHOES AND CANOES [by W: H: Giles Kingston: Lippincott, 1876]

"purports to describe the early days of a fur-trader in the Hudson's Bay Territory. It is an unpretentious narrativ, easily understood and certain to interest. We might compare it with Gerstaecker's works, but the English author has less imagination and a much less graphic style than his German prototype. In fact, we rather recommend the story for its apparent adherence to facts and the small quantity of romance in it. It has much to tell of hunters, trappers, voyageurs, and Indians, and the hardships of life, half a century ago, in the region now known as Manitoba." [Nation. 1955

ANSEL'S CAVE [by Albert Gallatin Riddle (1815-): Cleveland, Burrows, 1893] "is a story of early life in the 'Western Reserve,' opening in 1813, when these lands wer covered by a great forest, and communication with the outside world was throu an almost unbroken wilderness. The story was written twenty years ago, and because the personages go by their proper names, publication was delayed until the death of the principal actors and the dispersion of their descendants." [Critic. 1960

THEOPHILUS TRENT, or Old Times in the Oak Openings [by B: F. Taylor: Griggs, 1887] "is little more than a succession of scenes without life, without human interest and without the spirit of historical truth. Mr. Taylor has lost the true aspect of pioneer lift throu a sentimental feeling for the 'good old times'—or else the settlers of Michigan had a much easier time of it than did those of Illinois—and has only succeeded in producing a set of clever sketches." [Nation. 1965

1820-30

ZURY [by Jo. Kirkland: Houghton, 1887] "is a history, very simply and effectivly written, of the hardships undergone by the earlier settlers of Illinois." [Nation. 1970

THE McVEYS. [Same, 1888.] Continuation of above.—See No. 302. 1975

THE TRAVELLERS [by Catherine Maria Sedgwick: N. Y., 1825] "unites the interest of a fictitious narrativ with the description of real places and the memory of actual events. A family is represented as making the tour of Niagara, the lakes, Montreal, Quebec, &c. This affords an opportunity for describing places and local habits, which has been just sufficiently used. Some beautiful tho short descriptions of natural scenery occur, and a few romantic events." [U. S. Lit. Gazette. 1980

IN THE BOYHOOD OF LINCOLN. [by Hezekiah Butterworth: Appleton, 1892.] "The author calls it 'a true picture in a framework of fiction,' but it does not impress us as being a true picture of the boyhood of Lincoln. It has not the accent of reality which we find in the account which Herndon and Lamon giv of that boyhood, or even Hay and Nicolay, and this notwithstanding the fact that all which is best in the book, all which is vitally concerned with Lincoln, is lifted bodily from Herndon's book. That idealizing temper which gave us the cherry-tree Washington in Weems's Life and much subsequent biography, almost spoiling the Father of his Country for many of his children, is evidently at work on Lincoln. The most elaborate Life of him yet issued is written in the spirit of the statues of him in New York and Brooklyn which try to cover the actual man with tailor's clothes. Mr. Butterworth's representation of Lincoln's mother as 'a woman of deep inward experiences and subjectiv ideas,' also as a 'mystic.' wil perhaps cause those to smile who ar the best informed. The vehicle which Mr. Butterworth has chosen for his narrativ does not impress us as fortunate. The Tunker schoolmaster is an ineffable bore. Such a life as that of Lincoln can not, of course, be garded against the writer of fiction, but it must be one of the greatest who can improve upon the simple facts." [Nation.   1985

THE QUEEN OF THE SAVANNAH. [by Gustave Aimard: London, Ward, 1883.] "The principal events occur during the last and successful struggle for independence [1821]. Hence the gallant but ill-fated Iturbide, and the noble warrior-priest Sandoval, supply our author with an imposing bacground, while certain 'haciendcros' of the border, and Redmen and trappers from the wilderness, are the most prominent figures in the front." [Parthenon.   1990

1820-40.

DOCTOR JOHNS. [by Donald Grant Mitchell: Scribner, 1899.] "The period of which he writes dates from the war of 1812 and reaches forward to twenty years ago. It is a period of which Mr. Mitchell is wel informed. He draws upon memory,—not imagination, for his materials. He has attempted to giv the story of 'certain events in the life of an Orthodox Minister of Connecticut.' It is not exactly a narrativ of parish life, nor of public service; but starting from the humble parsonage in Ashfield, where Dr. Johns is the central figure, he weaves into the story from time to time such elements as set forth that home in all its features, and at the same time throes upon it enuf of the outside world to giv a good background for his portraits. There ar the Puritan minister in his austere theology; the Puritan spinster in her worldly primness; the good-natured sinner called the Squire; the sharp, shrewd deacons; the aristocratic families; the headquarters of Satan at the village tavern; the factotum of a country doctor; the sharp-visaged, dyspeptic clerical brethren of neboring towns; the varying beauty and pleasant quiet of a New England home. The author paints all this so that it stands before you. Mr. Mitchell has been compared to Irving in point of style, and there is ground for it. Both hav sunny, genial, cheerful temperaments; both liv in a leisurely growth of sentiments; both hav never stooped to the morbid sensations of the day. They ar pure, chaste, simple writers. They tel stories wel. They use the English language with the grace of a master; and they ar writers whom we ar tempted to undervalue for the peppery books of the hour." [Church Monthly.   1995

QUABBIN [by Fr. H: Underwood: Lee, 1893.] "is a cheerful, sympathetic story of life in New England, with its wonderful changes and transformation during the lapse of 60 years—the life-habits and dormant thôts, the changes which crept into the thôt of the settlement, and the broader views. The story is told in a charmingly simple manner, and yet the reader feels from the opening pages that the work is in the grasp of a master; that the subject is being treated by one who has himself studied every stage of the transformation. It is real life, most delightfully portrayed by a historian who is also a fascinating writer, which gives such a superior charm to 'Quabbin.'" [Arena.]—"Old New England towns used to be as much alike as peas in a pod, so in describing one of them patiently, faithfully, yet not uncritically. Mr. Underwood has done justice to all. Many of the towns stil ar there, looking about as they did before lands richer than any in New England coaxed the more enterprising farmers westward, and factories coaxed young men and women from old homesteads to town tenements; life in them, tho, is different, and it was principally to trace the changes in Yankee life, thot and manners that Mr. Underwood wrote his book. The story begins with Puritan days and ways, when the law as recorded in the Old Testament was as much in force as the law of the land, and the minister was the greatest man in the town. Folloing the people throu the incumbency of four successiv ministers, the author shos their chahge in material things as wel as in character. The narrativ is eminently readable; it is also accurate." [Godey's. 2000

SWALLOW BARN. [by J: P. Kennedy: Carey, 1832, Putnam, 1851.] "This is a series of most agreeable and faithful sketches of Virginia life. Twenty years ago it was read and enjoyed from the Chesapeake to the Ohio, and now a second generation wil read and enjoy it in a much more worthy and beautiful edition. We do not think that we praise it too hily in saying, that in after times, when the historian shal garner all the cotemporaneous material which he can find to represent, as it was, the social life of the Old Dominion in 1820, he wil value Swallow Barn above anything else in his possession." [So. Lit. Messenger.] —"Certain American institutions and modes of thot and feeling hav never been so wel described. We hav particular reference to the relation of master and slave, and the condition of the colored people in Virginia; and on this account especially we commend Swallow Barn to our reader's attention as exhibiting, in its true colors, a state of things which can never be bettered by all the efforts of all the abolitionists in the Union. The story of Abe, and the negro mother, for power and pathos, ar not surpassed by anything which has yet appeared in the literature of our country. As a collection of sketches Swallow Barn is hily creditable to Mr. Kennedy. One of the most clever and interesting parts of the work is the history of the famous Captain J: Smith, which, tho dragged in nec and heels for no conceivable purpos save to eke out quantity, is a romance in itself, which in the hands of Mr. Kennedy loses nothing of its importance." [New York Review. 2005

UNCLE TOM'S CABIN. [by Harriet (Beecher) Stowe: Boston, 1852.] "Its merit is not equal to its success, but it is a great novel. If examind as to the soundness of the political vues expressed in it, it may be declared very faulty and in some respects absurd; but all who read it as a novel ar hily delited with it. It has been objected to Uncle Tom that the author has misrepresented Southern life, and has gone beyond the proper sphere of the novelist and meddled with other people's business, when she holds up the slaveholders to the scorn of the world. These objections ar not good. It is not true that she has misrepresented Southern life. She has painted good and bad slaveholders, such men as there ar in every part of the world. She does not say or intimate that slaveholders ar worse than other men, but simply that they hav greater opportunities to do injustice. She selects extreme cases and extraordinary characters, as all novelists do. Neither is she wrong when she selects the horrors of

slavery as her subject." [Hesperian.]—
"Uncle Tom has many fine passages, but many more which ar crude in style and vulgar in tone: it has some real pathos, but much false sentiment: its negro characters ar very cleverly sketched, but they ar Northern, not Southern negroes; it exhibits much dramatic power, but little constructivness; its best points ar the humor and the characterization of its inferior personages. But as to being a book whose intrinsic merits justified its unparalleled sale in this country and in England, and the translation of it into all the languages of Europe, it is no such book. The admiration which it excited must be attributed entirely to two causes: the interest of the world in the subject on which it was written, and the fact that from the beginning to the end of it there is not a topic broached, not a sentence uttered which is not comprehensible by the most limited understanding, or an emotion uttered, a situation portrayed, which does not appeal directly to the sympathy of every heart however loly. If it be objected that this in itself implies a hi degree of merit, we reply, not necessarily; no more so than the fact that a cheap lithographer's windo with its 'loves' of little babies, its 'just breeched' boys, its 'sweet seventeen' girls, and its courageous firemen, is thronged all day, while the windo in which the works of Raphael, Titian, Delaroche, and Kaulbach ar to be seen, attracts but an occasional passenger, is proof of a hi degree of merit in the gaudy commonplace prints which appeal to crude, commonplace sympathy, throu associations altogether irrespectiv of art." [Albion. 2010

MIRAGE OF PROMISE. A [by Harriett Pennawell Belt: Lippincott, 1886] "is a beautifully written story of the early part of this century. It does not claim to be an historical romance, but much actual history is interwoven in it, and a vivid picture is given of the sufferings of abolitionists as well as slaves in the conflict which waged for so many years before the actual war. The scene in the hero's rooms when the mob threaten him, is a capital picture, and the entire story is a novel of vivid and picturesque effects illustrating the sternest truth, and certain therefore to give pleasure to both 'romantic' and 'realistic' readers." [Critic. 2015

HART AND HIS BEAR [by Albert Gallatin Riddle (1815-): Washington: Morrison, 1883] "has enuf of interest to cause one to forget in a measure the faulty diction. The descriptions of sounds and sights in the forest ar grafic, and sho a genuin love of nature, with considerable poetic feeling. Accounts of hunting and trapping ar numerous and in full detail. The story awakens sympathy. Portions of it ar exceedingly sad." [Nation.] Ohio. 2020

JUDITH. [by "Marion Harland," i. e., M., Virginia (Hawes) Terhune: Our Continent Pub. Co., 1884.] "A story from Marion Harland is a return upon old days when Mrs. Southworth and Mrs. Lee Hentz wer in fashion, as fashion in novels of that sort goes. Marion Harland told always a story full of incidents and of brave men and women. It was in short of the romantic school as that school was understood in the Old Dominion, but always pure and hi in motiv. The present 'Chronicle' is of fifty years ago, and made to include a much earlier time by stories within the story. Readers whose standard is set by the great novels wil not care at all for it, but the many who like a story because it is a story might do much worse than read this." [Nation. 2025

1830.

BUTTON'S INN [by Albion W. Tourgee (1838-): Roberts, 1887] " is a very mild and inexhaustiv story of the origin of Mormonism. The few pages of the preface, however, really contain more on this subject than all the rest of the book, and without these, perhaps many readers would hav failed to see in the Mormon chapters anything more than their bearing on the story. For the story itself has a genuin and wholesom interest, and one follows the fortunes of Dotty Button and her two worthy, generous lovers with a feeling which grows to be personal and warm-hearted." [Nation. 2030

1831.

THE OLD DOMINION. [by G: P. R. James: Harper, 1856.] Nat. Turner's Insurrection. 2035

1835.

AMBROSIO DE SETINEZ [by A. T. Myrthe: N. Y., Francis, 1842] " is the first Texan novel embracing a description of the countries bordering on the Rio Bravo, with incidents of the war of Independence." [Albion. 2040

INEZ, a tale of the Alamo, by Augusta J. Evans [Wilson]: Harper, 1855. 2045

REMEMBER THE ALAMO [by Amelia Edith (Huddleston) Barr (1833-): Dodd, 1888] " is a story which may be commended. Mrs. Barr is clever in selecting historical events more romantic and dramatic than most fiction, and in weaving instances of individual heroism. The episode of the revolt of American dwellers in Texas against Mexican rule affords her abundant material, which she uses to instruct the American youth concerning a small war of independence fôt in what has since become a part of his country, and to fire him with his forefathers' enthusiasm for ' liberty or death.' With such unimpeachable patriots as Davy Crockett and Sam Houston, such a bloody-minded villain as Santa Anna, and such thrilling events as the massacre of Goliad and the storming of the Alamo right at hand, there was small need of creating fictitious excitement." [Nation.]—According to catalog of Boston Pub. L'y, this book describes early Catholic missions in Florida [before Revolution]. 2050

1836-37.

OSCEOLA. [by Seymour R. Duke: N. Y., 1838.] Seminole War. 2055

1837.

THE PRISONER OF THE BORDER, by Ph. H. Meyers: N. Y., Derby, 1857. 2060

THE FAMILY WITHOUT A NAME, by Jules Verne: Low, 1890. 2065

1838.

THE GRAYSONS, [by E: Eggleston: N. Y., Century Co., 1888.] Illinois country life, youth of Lincoln.—See No. 40. 2070

MORE GOOD TIMES AT HACKMATACK [by M.. Prudence (Wells) Smith: Roberts, 1892] " is rather a series of sketches than a continued story of life in an inland (Mass.) village 60 years ago. The principal characters ar the children of the clergyman, and their occupations and amusements ar the theme of the book. They make sugar, go on a pic-nic, help raise the frame of the church, see a circus, enter heartily into the Tippecanoe political campaign—idolizing Webster, of course, whom they hear speak, as well as Everett—attend the academy, and finally one goes to Harvard. There ar few adventures, and those not of the thrilling kind, tho the children ar constantly falling into scrapes; but the interest of the book is wholly in its faithful pictures of a past generation. In these the author has shown much skill, and no little humor, especially in the description of the summer Sunday and of some of the more peculiar village characters." [Nation. 2075

1840.

THE HOOSIER SCHOOLMASTER. [by E: Eggleston: N. Y., Judd, 1872.] Indiana.—See No. 52. 2080

THE CIRCUIT RIDER. [by E: Eggleston: N. Y., Fords, 1874.] Indiana.—See No. 13. 2082

ROXY. [by E: Eggleston: N. Y., Scribner, 1878.] Indiana.—See No. 131. 2084

1843.

THE END OF THE WORLD. [by E: Eggleston: N. Y., Judd, 1872.] Indiana. Millerite excitement.—See No. 30. 2086

1844.

1844; or, the Power of the "S. F." [by T: Dunn English: N. Y., Stringer, 1847] "acquired a wide-spread celebrity, not only from its local interest, but from the vigor of its style and the faithfulness of its political details, and its graphic delineation of wel-known characters." [Albion. 2090

GARRET VAN HORN. [by J. S. Sauzade.] N. Y. 2095

1846-47.

JACK TIER, or the Florida Reef [by Ja. Fenimore Cooper: N. Y., Burgess, Stringer & Co., 1848] "has already appeared in Graham's Magazine, under the title of 'Rose Budd,' and it is advertised in London as Captain Spike. . . The story is one of nautical hazards and escapes, reminding the reader strongly of the Water Witch, as the same game of hide-and-seek is carried on throughout. The main charm rests rather on its narrativ and descriptiv portions, than on its delineations of character. Spike is the only personage whom the author has taken much pains to individualize— a man thoroly acquainted with all the practical part of his profession, cool in danger, never at a loss for resources in emergency, but crafty, hypocritical, avaricious, supremely selfish, vindictiv, and capable, without compunction, of deliberate murder. His character is wel and persistently portrayed, throughout the varied incidents of the tale, down to the fearful scene in which his career is suddenly brot to a close." [Literary World. 2100

1848-61.

HARRINGTON. [by W: D. O'Conor (-1889): Boston, Thayer, 1861.] "The introductory chapters, containing the flight of the slave Antony thru the Louisiana swamp, ar almost unequaled for unfaltering power and for gorgeous wealth of color. Many of the gloing sentences belong rather to passionate poetry than to tamer prose. The agonized resolution which turns the panting fugitiv's blood and body to fire,—the fear so vividly portrayed that the reader's nervs thril with the shoc which brings the hunted negro's heart almost to his mouth with one wild throb,—the matchless picture of the forest and marsh, lengthening and widening with dizzy swel to the weary eye and failing brain,—all ar the work of a master of language. When the scene shifts to Boston, the language, which was in perfect keeping with the tropical madness of

Antony's flight and the tropical splendor of the Southern forest, is extravagant to actual absurdity, when used with reference to ordinary scenes and ordinary events." [Atlantic. 2105

MY SOUTHERN FRIENDS. [by "Edmund Kirke," i. e., Ja. Roberts Gilmore (1823-): N. Y., Carleton, 1863.] "It is a novel of great, but unequal power. Its descriptions, both of scenery and character, ar clear and vivid, and there is much skill in the whole story. . . Selima, not Selma, Winchester was wel known in Cambridge, but there is much falsehood mingled with the common story of her short and sad life. She was the dauter of a slave, she was educated at the North, she returned to Tennessee and died there; thus far the story is true. But it is not true that her stepmother was the cause of her death, even remotely, nor did she die a slave, or of grief, or by her own hand." [Commonwealth. 2110

PECULIAR [by Epes Sargent: Boston, 1864: new ed., 1892] "takes its name from the hero, a slave. Mr. Sargent believed in calling a spade a spade; hence some of the passages ar harroing, however satisfactory is the end. To those who passed throu the war times, this book is an interesting reminder; while to those of this generation, for whom those times ar a tradition, it shos in brilliant colors pages of American history which wil be always a mingling of glory and shame. As a tale, 'Peculiar' is absorbing; as history, it is in essentials true, giving references for the most improbable of the statements, that the reader may see for himself. We who ar hero-worshipers ar sorry to be reminded that Carlyle, Ruskin, Maury and Gladstone wer once supporters of slavery and that Gladstone inherited wealth gained from the Liverpool slave-trade. . . The plot is intricate, the situation touching." [Commonwealth. 2115

WASH BOLTOR, M. D. [Cincinnati, Clark, 1872.] "In the narrativ of Wash Boltor's life it would appear to be the author's design to illustrate the career of the average American politician. The scene of action is laid in Boshville, under which designation there is but little difficulty in recognizing Cincinnati. The name of the hero might as wel hav been candidly spelt Bolter, for he was always found vociferous in the party which was in a position to command and besto office. Some of Boltor's oratory goes to vindicate this erratic course. To literary polish the work has no claim. The writer is evidently familiar with the American political stump-speech, and the defence of slavery he puts into one of Boltor's speeches is a model of its kind. One passage runs thus: 'These blac nomads wer living in idleness, with no other mission under heaven than to kil and be killed, eat and be eaten, to be the sport of their own blac princes, or a bonne bouche for a hungry lion or hippopotamos. In Africa they wer neither useful nor ornamental; they had no arts or sciences, and in mechanical knoledge wer far belo a beaver or a Digger Indian. To make a long story short, the trader in his capacity of purveyor to the world, whether it be ice from the North Pole or coal from the Equator (for it generally happens that nature puts the things precisely where they ar not wanted), bròt, among his spices, gums, and nuts, to America, a sample of these blac aborigines. And thus these blac nomads, from leading an idle and useless life in a menagerie, wer elevated to be co-laborers of a civilization which wears clean linen and believes in the Bible and the divine right of labor." [Nation. 2120

SALTILLO BOYS [by W: Osborn Stoddard: Harper, 1882] "is a pleasant story, the scene being a town in central New York 30 years ago. The boys described ar from 13 to 16 and belong to a school in which the master endeavors to impress the value of self-government upon his pupils. This lesson is fairly wel brôt out in the various incidents given of life in and out of school." [Nation. 2125

HOT PLOWSHARES [by Albion W. Tourgée: N. Y., Ford, 1883] "covers the period from the election of Taylor to the outbreak of the civil war. According to the preface, 'it is designed to giv a revue of the anti-slavery struggle, by tracing its growth and the influence of the sentiment upon contrasted characters.' The book is too long and too diffuse for any vivid effect." [Nation. 2130

ON NEWFOUND RIVER. [by T: Nelson Page: Scribner, 1891.] "The author takes his reader into the pleasant scenery of a Virginia plantation, but before the story closes, the quiet of the woods, the old mil-pond and the river-bottoms is broken by some very exciting events. The plot turns upon the indomitable, hereditary wil of the Landons, in whom race qualities sho a remarkable persistence. 'Tall, strait, keen-eyed, aquiline, they grew, father and son for generation after generation, as distinct from their plain nêbors on Newfound as a Lombardy poplar is from the common pine.' The family temper, which has already cost a master of the 500 negroes and the acres an heir, threatens to bring about a tragedy between 'the Major' and his only son, Bruce. But the story is, in the end, one of averted consequences and unexpected restoration. The Major and the Perdita-like heroin, happy among her old books, her hollyhocs and sweet-peas, and cheering her aged grandfather with feminin wiles, fall into rather hacneyed theatrical attitudes on their first meeting in the thicket. The characters, in fact, which ar found to be always true to the life, ar those of the plain nêbors on Newfound." [Nation. 2135

DOWN THE O-HI-O. [by C: Humphrey Roberts: McClurg, 1892.] "The reader must not suppose that this is a book of cheap jocularity. On the contrary, tho a story in form, and one of some merit even as a story, its real value is in a series of scenes, often felicitous, and sometimes extremely spirited, of rural life, chiefly among Quakers, on the north bank of the Ohio in the period shortly before the war. The writer may wel hav been part of what he saw, and tho there is a careless manner about some of his narrativ, and he is more or less artificial in his treatment of the plot and the lawyers who ar needed by it, his genuin interest in the more simple parts, as, for example, in the capital racing scene, carries the reader as wel as the writer along at a good pace." [Atlantic. 2140

CHILDREN OF DESTINY. [by Molly Elliot Seawell: Appleton, 1893.] "The author apparently doubts the determinativ influence of character for good or il, or at all events believes it to be subject to Ananke assuming the form of a family doom. Her chief figure is Mr. Richard Skelton, a Virginian land and slave-owner, born 70 years ago and fortunately able to enjoy his property without any question of right or righteousness. Skelton is rather an interesting person, of marked individuality, but we cannot let ourselvs go with him heartily, because, from sundry hints, we hav gathered that, at the moment when we should most wish him to abide with us, he wil, in accordance with family precedent, depart for another world. If one can forget the impending catastrophe, there is much to enjoy in the delineation of unusual characters and in the pictures of social life. Miss Seawell has probably grasped pretty exactly the kind of splendor which prevailed in the splendid old South, and which has dazzled the eyes of so many enthusiastic and imaginativ chroniclers. The penalty of perpetual lotus-eating is intellectual and spiritual death; and when we ar invited to consider what the slaveholding aristocracy had not, we ar less moved to envy what it had or to exaggerate its magnificence." [Nation. 2145

IN OLE VIRGINIA. [by T: Nelson Page: Ward, Lock, 1893.] "These stories enshrine whatever was best in the old slavery days. Picturing the patriarchal life in the Southern States, where the virtues of kindliness, devotedness, and gratitude had a not unfriendly soil to gro in, they ar nevertheless not one-sided. They contain grim suggestions of the facts which wer painted broadly in 'Uncle Tom's Cabin.' Mr. Page's Southern patriotism is reasonable, and his power of winning sympathy for his point of vue undoubted." [Bookman. 2150

IOLA LEROY. [by Frances E. W. Harper: Phil'a, Garrigues, 1893.] "The present generation can hardly be reminded too often of what slavery was. . . . 'Iola Leroy' tels again the shameful story, and brings the scene throu the war days into the times of her education and professional callings for the colored people. The book derives added interest from being written by one of the race, long known as an ardent worker in the cause of her people." [Nation. 2155

RACHEL STANWOOD. [by Lucy Gibbons Morse: Houghton, 1894.] "The old-time flavor of this story will delight many thousands of people who ar not yet old. The scenes are laid in New York, and the time antedates the civil war by a few years—a time when 'the best people' knew one another, and did not divide into cliques the boundaries of which consist principally of bank accounts. Rachel Stanwood is dauter of a couple of charming Quakers who ar liked by all of their acquaintances, yet suspected by some, for they are of the dreadful set known as 'abolitionists,' and the underground railway is believed to hav a large station somewhere in the Stanwoods' bacyard. An indignant slave-owner visits the house in quest of some human property, and givs the author a chance to sho how much and fairly the harborer of fugitiv slaves could talk without lying and also without giving information. Among the characters ar W: Lloyd Garrison and Wendell Phillips, and there is much political talk peculiar to the time, as wel as a lot of love-making between entirely natural and interesting people. The book reads more like a series of recollections than a work of fiction, tho the tale is interesting and romantic." [Godey's. 2160

1857.

NEIGHBOR JACKWOOD. [by J: T. Trowbridge: N. Y., Sheldon, 1858.] Vermont. Enforcement of Fugitive Slave Law.—See No. 93 and Atlantic Monthly, March, 1895. 2165

TRUE WOMANHOOD. [by J: Neal: Ticknor, 1859.] "The scene is New York during the great revival of 1857-58, and much use is made of the wel-known incidents of that time. The author shows his warm sympathy with the religious excitement which then swept over a large part of the Christian world, by repeating many of the arguments by which it was urged and vindicated, and by bringing nearly all of his dramatis personæ under its influence. . . . The conversations and discussions in which the book abounds are lited with allusions to many topics of general interest. Among them are the commercial crisis, the question of 'Woman's Rights,' the dramatic element of the Bible, and the 'garroting' mania. A marked preference for English habits in social life appears from time to time." [North Am. Review. 2170

THE MYSTERY OF METROPOLISVILLE. [by E: Eggleston: N. Y., Judd, 1873.] Minnesota.—See No. 92. 2180

JOHN GODFREY'S FORTUNES. [by Bayard Taylor: Putnam, 1864.] New York. Literary life.—See No. 280. 2175

DR. SEVIER. [by G: W. Cable: Boston, 1884.] New Orleans.—See No. 234. 2185

1860.

AMONG THE PINES. [by "Edmund Kirke": N. Y., Carleton, 1862.] S. C. 2190

1861-65.

THE PARTISAN LEADER. [by " E: W. Sidney ": Washington, Caxton, 1836.] "The scene is laid in Virginia, near the close of the year 1849. By a long series of encroachments by the federal government on the rights and powers of the states, our federativ system is supposed to be destroyed, and a consolidated government, with the forms of a republic and the powers of a monarchy, to be established on its ruins. The various steps by which this great change has been effected ar pointed out, partly in actual detail, and partly by inference from the incidents narrated. Mr. Van Buren is supposed to be at the end of his third presidential term, to hav been just elected for the fourth time, and to hav garded himself, not only by activ and submissiv tools at his 'court' at Washington, and in all the offices in the country, but also by a strong army devoted to his service. The southern states, with the exception of Virginia, hav seceded and formed a confederacy among themselvs. Virginia, however, has theretofore been kept in subjection, chiefly by the artful management of certain small politicians, to whom accidental circumstances hav given influence, and the means of deceiving the people. Yet even Virginia, at the date of the story, has shaken off her lethargy and become sensible of the necessity of uniting herself with her sister states of the south." [So. Lit. Messenger.

—— SAME, by Nath. Beverley Tucker (1784-51): N. Y., Carleton, 1864. 2195

CUDJO'S CAVE [by J. T. Trowbridge: Boston, Tilton, 1864] "is a spiritedly written tale. 'Cudjo' is a runaway slave, and his 'Cave' is among the mountains of Tennessee. We hav perils, escapes, and flights; and it would appear that all those in Tennessee who had Northern proclivities, whether white or blac, wer hunted down like wild beasts. One poor schoolmaster gets tarred and feathered, and whipping white women seems not altogether uncommon. The descriptions ar all excellent." [Reader.]—"The plot is wel conceived and sustained, and the interest never flags from the first page to the last. There is no dul reading in the book, no interminable preludes or introductions. The hero is a young schoolmaster, and a real hero he proves himself in his gentleness, conscientiousness, and manly moral and physical courage. Carl, the German boy, is an inimitable picture of young German life and character. Toby, the house negro, is, in his mingled stupidity, cunning, and faithfulness, drawn to the life. Nor ar the negroes of the cave less excellent. Events hurry forward, different characters are strangely grouped, new elements and capacities constantly developed, while truth to the original conception is constantly adhered to. Graphic descriptions and picturesque situations abound." [Continental. 2200

OLD JACK AND HIS FOOT CAVALRY. [N. Y., Bradburn, 1864.] "This is called a story of the war in the Old Dominion, but is a 'Southside' view of the contest. 'Old Jack' is said to be a term of endearment used by the soldiers of Stonewall Jackson's brigade toard their commander, and the 'Foot Cavalry' ur his infantry brigade, so called from their fleetness of foot. It is a gloing description of the prowess and religious nobility of Jackson, and brightly gilds the deeds of the Virginia soldiery." [Commonwealth. 2205

AMONG THE GUERILLAS, by "Edmund Kirke": N. Y., Carleton, 1866. 2210

THE BROWNINGS. [by J.. G. Fuller: N. Y., Dodd, 1867.] Country life in Confederacy. 2215

MISS RAVENEL'S CONVERSION from Secession to Loyalty. [by J: W: DeForest: Harper, 1868.] "It is long since we hav met a book which has presented to us so many amusing people; the author has the art of lavishing goodness upon his favorits without making them insipid, while he justly gibbets the mean and the vicious, and shows the weakness of vice. The great events of the war contribute their quota of amusement, and furnish abundance of incidents, telling situations, startling sensations, without the necessity in any instance of having recourse to a strained effect or improbable adventure." [Examiner. 2220

HILT TO HILT, by J: Esten Cooke: N. Y., Carleton, 1869. 2225

HAMMER AND RAPIER. [by J: Esten Cooke: N. Y., Carleton, 1870.] "The author has essayed to giv, in a somewhat fanciful and romantic style and from the Confederate standpoint, a history of the war in Virginia. He is master of an easy and graphic style, altho it sometimes verges upon the turgid and grandiose, and he writes with a warmth of feeling which attracts sympathy if it does not always assure assent. Those who like to think Lee the ablest of generals, and Stonewall Jackson the loftiest of heroes, wil find 'Hammer and Rapier' a book after their hearts. It is just to ad that tho a Virginian and a Confederate soldier, Mr. Cooke tries hard, and often successfully, to do justice to the aims and purposes of the North; and unlike some who hav written in the same interest, he is always gentlemanly, and never acrimonious." [Hearth & Home. 2230

CAPTAIN PHIL. [by M. M. Thomas: Holt, 1884.] "The hero is an orphan lad who accompanies his older brother during the whole of the war. He is present at the first battle of Bull Run. Afterwards he joins the Western army, under Rosecrans, remains with it during the pursuit, first of Bragg and afterwards of Johnson, and is in the battles of Shiloh, Murfreesboro, and Chickamauga, and in the march to the sea. All the phases of camp life, its humors and its hardships, the peculiarities of the different men, their talk, their songs, their heroism, often their simple piety, ar represented with a graphic force and truthfulness worthy of great praise. Scattered throu the book ar incidents, almost every one of which, Mr. Thomas assures us, 'is a real experience,' of courage and devotion displayed on the battlefield, and especially after the battle, in rescuing or in succoring the wounded. Equally wel done ar the descriptions of the contrabands and the poor whites, and the scenery of the country throu which the army passd." [Nation. 2235

THE STORY OF DON MIFF [by Virginius Dabney, Lippincott, 1886] "is wel worth reading. It is a story of Virginia, and much of it is remarkably wel told. . . . There ar chapters in the diffuse narrativ of such interest, and frequent passages so really eloquent and dramatic, that we commend the book to our readers with the full confidence that they wil find it repay perusal. They wil discover, at any rate, that they can skip a very large part of it without the slightest prejudice to the rest." [Southern Bivouac. 2240

IN WAR TIMES AT LA ROSE BLANCHE [by M. E. M. Davis: Boston, Lothrop, 1888] "stands among the best of the liter war books in its graphic pictures of plantation life, from a strictly domestic point of vue—even from a nursery standpoint; for it is a child's observation and experience and memory which giv form to these charming sketches—a child who sees her young brothers go off to the war, and who sits upon the fence to wave them a goodbye as they march down the lane; who sees the work of the sugar plantation devolving on her mother's shoulders; who finds that a Yankee boy among those encamped on the lawn can 'play ladies' with her and make delightful wooden dolls. An unaffected pathos and simplicity make these pages seem, not descriptions but experiences; the figures which move throu them, old and young, blac and white, liv and hav a veritable being. The whole book, in its truth and tenderness, is like one of its pictures—a morning-glory groing on a soldier boy's grave." [Nation. 2245

TWO LITTLE CONFEDERATES [by T: Nelson Page: Scribner, 1888] "is a most natural, pleasing, and at times touching story. The scene is laid in a plantation in Virginia, and the adventures described ar those of two boys who, tho too young to join the army, yet come freely in contact with the excitement, anxiety, privation and sorro which war entails." [Nation. 2250

JED. [by Warren Lee Goss: Boston, Crowell, 1889.] "In some respects this is the best boys' book about the Civil War we ever read. The hero, a Massachusetts lad who, having been a drummer-boy before the war, wins his shoulder-straps by faithful service and falls in one of the last skirmishes, is a manly fello with a noble spirit, of whom no boy can read without being the better for it. There is an air of truthfulness about the book, also, which confirms the author's statement that the incidents narrated ar real ones. The description of Andersonville is an unusually powerful piece of writing, while the account of the escape of Jed and his companions possesses a thrilling interest." [Nation. 2255

WITH LEE IN VIRGINIA. [by G: Alfred Henty: Scribner, 1889.] "The author has succeeded not merely in making an entertaining tale full of exciting incident, but also in giving some local color to it. His hero takes part only in the battles in which the Confederates wer victors, as Bull Run, Fredericksburg, and Chancellorsville." [Nation. 2260

JACK HORNER. [by M. F. [S.] Tiernan: Houghton, 1890.] Life in Richmond, 1864-65.—See No. 760. 2265

ADVENTURES OF A FAIR REBEL. [by "Matt Crim": N. Y., Webster, 1891.] "The plot has often done service in stories of the Civil War, but it still recommends itself, for its construction follos the lines of nature. A Southern girl meets her destiny in the shape of a young Federal officer, who saves her and her companions from the hands of freebooters while traveling throu the mountains of North Carolina to Georgia. Desperate complications arise, not only from the fact that Rachel herself is an ardent rebel, but because the family of Captain Lambert, who received his mental and moral training at the North, among his father's relativs, ar living in Georgia, and ar heart and soul with the Confederacy. These complications ar gradually untangled by the force of circumstances. In fact, toards the last, there is a weakening in the working out of the plot, so that almost too much is left to circumstances. But the style is simple and straitforward, with fine touches here and there. The two old negroes, 'Uncle Ned' and 'Aunt Milly,' ar very lifelike, having none of the exaggerations which often make such portraiture mere caricature. The shoing forth of the best aspects on both sides of the dreadful struggle is skilfully done, avoiding false sentiment, and maintaining an almost judicial tone, which does not, however, lessen the interest of the story." [Nation. 2270

1861-5.

AMONG THE CAMPS. [by T: Nelson Page: Scribner, 1891.] "Each story has reference to some incident of the war. A vein of mingled pathos and humor runs throu them and greatly hitens their charm. It is the early experience of the author himself, doubtless, which makes his pictures of life in a Southern home during the great struggle so vivid and truthful. There is none of the bitterness of the contest, however, to be perceived in the book, as the author has wisely chosen incidents in which Confederate and Union soldiers meet only to do some kindness to a child." [Nation. 2275

ON THE PLANTATION. [by Joel Chandler Harris: Appleton, 1892.] "The autobiographic character of this book invests it with peculiar interest. The sub-title calls it 'a story of a Georgia boy's adventures during the war,' and it is really a valuable, if modest, contribution to the history of the war within the Confederate lines, particularly on the eve of the catastrophe. While Mr. Harris in his preface professes to hav lost the power to distinguish between what is true and what is imaginativ in his episodical narrativ, the reader readily finds the clue, and it is instructiv to notice how 'Uncle Remus'' humor is robbed of its contagiousness when the tale is about a funny incident in his own experience which he is too conscientious to embellish. The history of the plantation, the printing-office, the blac runaways and white deserters of whom the impending break-up made the community tolerant, the coon and foxhunting, forms the serious purpos of the book, and holds the reader's interest from beginning to end. Like 'Daddy Jake,' this is a good anti-slavery tract in disguise, and does credit to Mr. Harris' humanity." [Examiner. 2280

1869-73.

HONEST JOHN VANE. [by J: W: De Forest: New Haven, Patten, 1875.] Politics in Washington.—See No. 270. 2285

JUSTINE'S LOVERS. [by J: W: De Forest: Harper, 1878.] Politics in Washington.—See No. 284. 2290

As collateral reading:—

YOUNG FOLKS' HISTORY OF THE WAR [by J: Denison Champlin (1834-): Holt, 1881] "can be heartily recommended. Indeed, the book gives a great deal more than it promises, for it is equally wel adapted to general readers. It is, in short, a wel written and entertaining history, fair and impartial in tone and aiming rather at incident and graphic narrativ than at political and strategic analysis, altho these ar not neglected; affording, therefore, probably as good an account of these events as most wil desire. It is copiously illustrated as wel with maps and plans, as with portraits, vues, and pictures of special objects of interest. Few or none of the illustrations ar 'made-up' pictures. There is an index." [Nation.

THE CIVIL WAR [by Mrs. C. E. Cheney: Estes, 1883] "can be heartily recommended. The first few pages strike one as being rather stif and artificial in style, and altogether there is too great tendency toards digression and 'moralizing.' The story, however, is exceedingly wel told, and in a spirit of keen sympathy with the objects and results of the war, if at times a little intolerant in tone." [Nation. 2295

MEMORIALS OF A SOUTHERN PLANTER [by Susan (Dabney) Smedes: Baltimore, Cushing, 1887] "is a little book which may interest the English reader by its pictures of plantation life. It is a memoir, composed chiefly of home letters, of a member of an old Virginian family, who tho a successful tobacco cultivator in his State, was determind by circumstances to migrate to the cotton-raising districts. The round of life under the planter's sway is vividly delineated in the family correspondence, and the recollections of an old servant, known as 'Mammy Harriet,' present a lively picture of the journey down South. References to politics and the war ar frequent." [Saturday Review. 2300

1863-67.

CROWN JEWELS. [by Emma L. Moffett: N. Y., Carleton, 1871.] Mexico. 2305

1865.

FIVE HUNDRED MAJORITY, or the Days of Tammany. [by Wyllis Niles: Putnam, 1872.] "A disgraceful record of a disgraceful time." [Nation. 2310

1886.

THE EARTH TREMBLED [by E: Payson Roe: Dodd, 1887] "describes the Charleston earthquake wel and vividly, and without dwelling too painfully on its horrors, brings them home to all by their influence on the natures and fortunes of his characters... The characters ar strongly drawn, and the comedy-relief is excellent. Altho the thread of the story is twisted out of the sectional hatred which stil survived, there is nothing in it to offend either Northern or Southern sympathizers." [Epoch. 2315

From W: M. Griswold, 25 Craigie St., Cambridge, Mass.

TRAVEL, 3 vols., each $2.25; the same matter re-arranged by Countries—France, Germany, Italy, Switzerland, each $1.25; discount on two copies (ordered at same time), 10 per cent, on three, 12⅓, on four, 16⅔, on five, 20.

PART I., Novels of American Country Life, New (1893) edition, 96 pages, $ .75 (or exchanged for first edition and $ .25.), —— 2 copies of same Part [ordered at same time] $1.12; three, $1.50; five, $2.50; ten, $3.75; PART II., Novels of American City Life; III., International Novels, price: $ .50 each; (two copies, $ .75, —— three, $1.; —— four, $1.25; —— five, $1.50, —— six, $4., —— ten, $5.); IV., Romantic Novels, $1.00 (2 copies $1.50, ten, $5.); V., British Novels, $2.00 (2 copies, $1.50); VI., Novels descriptive of Life in France, $1.00; VII., —— of Germany, $1.00; VIII., —— of Italy, $ .25 (2 copies, $ .37); IX., —— of Russia, $ .50; X., —— of Norway, $ .25.

Parts I-X bound in cloth, $8.: — 2 copies, $13.
HISTORICAL Novels, Part I. (*ANCIENT LIFE*), $ .50.
——, ——, Part II., (*NORTH-AMERICA*). $1.

Opinions of Librarians.

FROM A NORWICH [CONN.] PAPER.

Librarian Trumbull has placed upon the catalogue table four little volumes designed to help searchers for interesting books in the domain of fiction. They are entitled respectively, Romantic, International, English, American City and American Country Life novels, and are brief digests of standard stories under these heads, prepared by W. M. Griswold.

Any person looking for a good novel is not obliged to depend solely upon the title for a guide, but in a few lines gets a idea of the gist of the story. If the book be in the library its number is indicated in red on the margin. The scheme is both clever and helpful.

FROM THE AMSTERDAM [N. Y.] PUB. LIBRARY.

"I have been several times asked such questions as 'Is the library to be a high-toned affair, admitting only such works as the critics of the Nation and Saturday Review approve of, or will it contain also the sort of novels which meet the approval of factory 'hands,' whose literary opinions are quite as pronounced as those of any critic of them all?'... In the choice of volumes, the opinions of competent critics will, of course, have due weight, but the likes and dislikes of the average citizen will be consulted also. The library, it is hoped, will contain plenty of the best literature for those who desire the best. By means, too, of critical journals and Griswold's DESCRIPTIVE LISTS OF NOVELS, opportunity will be given to those who desire to cultivate in themselves a liking for the best. But, on the other hand, any sort of literature (not absolutely vicious) is probably better than no literature at all. And so if John Doe and Richard Roe want their Rider Haggard, the book committee will doubtless see to it that their Rider Haggard they shall get, altho the book committee may themselves strongly sympathize with the very tired English writer who has pictured to himself the New Jerusalem as the place where the "Rudyards cease from Kipling and the Haggards Ride no more."—*Ed. in Amsterdam (N. Y.) Daily Democrat, 7 Dec., '91.*

FROM THE BROOKLYN Y. M. C. A. LIBRARY.

"Please send us Four copies. Your effort is a heavy task, but the result, I believe, will be lasting and appreciated. Hope it may be followed by many other lists."

FROM THE BUFFALO LIBRARY.

"Your excellent lists are most useful library aids."

FROM THE CLEVELAND PUBLIC LIBRARY.

"I think your lists will prove very valuable to our readers."

FROM THE PEORIA PUBLIC LIBRARY.

"Please send me Three copies, and the same number of any list of books containing descriptive or critical notes, that you may publish. I want one to bind and preserve and two to cut up and paste on catalogue cards for our classified catalogue."

FROM THE ST. LOUIS PUBLIC LIBRARY.

"You are doing a valuable work. Hope you will keep on extending in this line."

FROM WEYMOUTH (MASS.) PUBLIC LIBRARY.

"Please send us Fifteen copies of List. We have examined it and feel sure that it will be of help to our borrowers." [After experimenting with first List, 10 copies each of second and third Lists were ordered.]

From Authors and Editors.

FROM W. D. HOWELLS.

"I am delighted with the notion of your list of Novels about Country Life in America, and I think you have most charmingly realized it. The book will be useful to every book-lover and critic and librarian. Now that it satisfies it, I know that I have always felt the need of just such a list." FROM SARAH ORNE JEWETT :— 'You have certainly made a most attractive pamphlet." FROM AGNES REPPLIER :— "A most useful and entertaining little book." FROM J. T. TROWBRIDGE :— "You are doing admirable work for American literature." FROM PROF. W. DWIGHT WHITNEY :— "I shall often dip into it [No. 5.] with much interest."

"We are inclined to christen Mr. Griswold the friend of all who have much to do with books. ... Each title is followed with a brief analysis of the story. It is these compact and characteristic analyses which give this work its unique value. They involve an enormous amount of reading, and do what few catalogs attempt at all, and none carry as far,—they tell the reader what the book is."—*The Independent.*

"It may be feared that publishers will scarcely approve of the compiler's attempt to 'lessen the disposition to read inferior new books,' while the ever increasing body of authors engaged in the production of such books will look upon his endeavors with even less favour. Still, anything that will keep people from reading—and newspaper critics from praising—inferior new books is to be welcomed."—*Dundee Advertiser.*

"... Many of these books are typical, or have a historic value; some of them are of the first quality of excellence, and should not be allowed to perish at least in the present age; and all are worthy of the place given them."—*Popular Science Monthly.*

"Every library, at least, should possess itself of the List. ... It is an attempt, in behalf of rational reading, to restore to novels their novelty—i. e., to save from unjust oblivion such as have grown old without ceasing to be good and profitable."—*Nation.*

"It is a collection of brief critical notices from various journals, intended to give as good an idea as possible of each book, and covering books of date as far back as 1849. The object, indeed, is partly to recall the good books of years gone by. The pamphlet is by no means bad reading, giving one many of the pleasures of reminiscence." —*American.*

"Of all Mr. Griswold's valuable work this promises to be most useful to the general public." —*Publisher's Weekly.*

INDEX

—TO—

Authors, Titles, Scenes, Characters and Events Described.[*]

Abbott, E. A., author of Philochristus, H253
Abolitionists in Mirage of Promise, H RachelStanwood, H 2160
Acadia, scene of Evangeline, H 1030
Ackerman, A. W., author Price of Peace, H47
Adam, G. M., author of Algonquin Maiden, H
Adams, Mrs. J:, Letters, H 1637
Adams, J. T. author of Lost Hunter, H 730
Adrian H 1735
Adventures of Capt. Mago, H41
Adventures of a Fair Rebel, H 2270
Aenone, H380
Agamenticus, H 1085
Agathonia, H525
Agnes, H 1600
Agnes Surriage, H 1005
Agrippina, character in Empress, H295
Great Empress, H300
Aimard, G., author of Queen of the Savannah
Alaric, character in Antonina, H495
Alda, H310
Alden, J:, character in Standish, H 670
Alexandria, scenes in Hypatia, H500
Thorny Path, H420
Algerine Captive, H 920
Algonquin Maiden, H 1075
Alkibiades, character in Aspasia, H110
Charmione, H115
Philothea, H100
Allen, Ethan, char. in Ethan Allen, H 1245
Rangers, H 1240

Amasis, character in Daughter Egyptian King, H80
Ambrosio de Setinez, H 2040
Among the Camps, H 2275
Among the Guerillas, H 2210
Among the Pines, H 2190
Amphitheatre, scenes in Antinous, H385
Darkness and Dawn, H325
Gladiator, H410
Gladiators, H335
Amymone, H105
Anaxagoras, character in Aspasia, H110
Anchorites, described in Homo Sum, H460
Andre, Major, char. in Pemberton, H 1460
Colonial Doorways, H
Ansel's Cave, H 1960
Antinous, H385
Antinous, character in Emperor, H395
Antonina, H495
Apelles, H140
Aphrodite, H90
Arius the Libyan, H465
Army life described in Capt. Phil, H 2235
Arnold, Benedict, char. in Grace Dudley, H 1290
Great Treason, H 1625
Pemberton, H 1460
Rejected Wife, H 1180
Asia Minor coast, scenery Aphrodite, H90
Aspasia, H110
Aspasia, character in Amymone, H105
Aspasia, H110
Philothea, H100

Assyria, history in Azeth, H55
Sarchedon, H50
Atala, H 610
Athanasius, character in Last Athenian, H455
Athenian, see Last Athenian, H455
Athenian Letters, H120
Atherstone, Edwin, author of, Handwriting on the Wall, H70
Attila, H510
Augustus, character in Dion, H285
Aulnay, character in Aurelian, H 444
Austin, J: (G.), author of Betty Alden, H 735
Desmond Hundred, 21
Dr. Le Baron, H 855
Mrs. Beau. Brown, 89
Nameless Noblemen, H
Standish of Standish, H
Azeth, the Egyptian, H55
Babylon, history in Life and Travels of Herodotus, H95
Master of the Magicians, H60
Bachelor of Salamanca, H 815
Bacon, Delia, author of Tales of the Puritans,
Bacon, Nat., character in Cavaliers of Va., H 860 Hansford, H 870
Baldwin, J:, author of Story of the Golden Age, H35
Balestier, W., author of Victorious Defeat, H 1745
Bandits of the Osage, H 1865

[*] The numbers refer to the Notice of the book, not to the page on which it is found. When "H" precedes the number, this indicates that the notice is in the Historical Series.

1

INDEX.

Banks of the Ohio, H 1606
Barclay, L;, author of Personal Recollections, H 1605
Barr, A. E. (H.), author Between Two Loves, 1103
Bow of Orange Ribbon, Daughter of Fife, 1186
Jan Vedder's Wife, 761
Master of His Fate, 1534
Remember the Alamo, H
Squire of Sandalside, 1805
Barthelemy, J. J., author Travels of Anacharsis,
Bathsheba, character in Fair to Look Upon, H44
Battles, naval, described in Israel, Potter
Midshipman Paulding, H
Miles Wallingford, H
Pilot, H 1400
Zachary Phipps, H 1835
Bay Path, H 705
Beach, R. G., author of Puritan and Quaker, H
Beauchampe, H 1710
Becker, W: A., author of Charicles, H135
Gallus, H225
Begum's Daughter, H 910
Behemoth, H 530
Bellingham, R:, char. in Penelope's Suitors, H 995
Woman of Shawmut, H
Belshazzar, character in Handwriting on the Wall, H70
Belt, H. P., author of Mirage of Promise, H
Ben Hur, H250
Bennett, Em., author of Bandits of the Osage, Traitor, H 1815
Bennett, G. J., author of Empress, H295
Berkeley, W:, character in Cavaliers of Va., H 860
Betrothed of Wyoming, H 1350
Betty Alden, H 735
Bird, Ro. M., author of Calaver, H 545
Hawks of Hawk-Hollow, H 1520
Infidel, H 550
Nick of the Woods, H
Black, E. J., author of Caecilia Metella, H190
Blackbeard, H 985

Black-plumed Rifleman, H 1550
Black Watch, H 1235
Blanche of Brandywine, H 1285
Bogart, W: H:, author of Life of Boone, H 1720
Bonnybel Vane, H 1220
Boone, Life of, H 1720
Boston, scenes in
Days of Cocked Hats, H 900
Fair Puritan, H 895
Harrington, H 2105
Hobomok, H 690
Hundred Boston Orators, H 1640
Lionel Lincoln, H 1230
Nix Mate, H 800
Penelope's Suitors, H
Rebel, H 1185
Traits of the Tea-party, Woman of Shawmut, H
Young Folk's Hist. Bos.
Bow of Orange Ribbon, H 1027
Boys and Girls of Revolution, H 1612
Boys' and Girls' Plutarch, H 143
Boys' and Girls' Herodotus, H 97
Brace, J: P., author of Fawn of Palefaces, H
Brackenridge, H. H., Modern Chivalry, H 1765
Bradford, gov. W:, char. in Peep at Pilgrims, H 740
Bradshaw, J:, author of Raphael Ben Isaac
Brandon, H 1060
Brant, character in Greyslaer, H 1360
Mary Derwent, H 1380
Bravo's Daughter, H 1430
Breck, S:, Recollections, H 1795
Bride of the Nile, H505
Brooks, E. S., author of In Leisler's Time, H 905
Son of Issachar, H257
Brownings, the, H 2215
Bubastes,
Cat of Bubastes, H10
Buckingham, H. S.,
Harry Burnham, H 1580
Bulwer, see Lytton
Bunce, O. B., author of Romance of the Rev., H
Bunker-Hill in
Israel Potter, H 1415
Lionel Lincoln, H 1230
Buntline, Ned, author of

Red Revenger, H 960
Burdette, C:, author of Margaret Moncrieff, H
Burr, A., character in Conspirator, H 1820
Guert Ten Eyck, H
Margaret Moncrieff, H
Minister's Wooing, H
Rivals, H 1805
Traitor, H 1815
Victim of Intrigue, H
Zachary Phipps, H 1835
Burton, or the Sieges, H 1255
Butt, B. M., author of Delicia, 1197
Elizabeth, 681
Eugenie, 2023
Geraldine Hawthorne, H
Hester, 2064
Miss Molly, 1559
Butterworth, H., author Boyhood of Lincoln, H
Up from the Cape, 394
Young Folk's Hist. Boston, H 1210
Buttons Inn, H 2030
Buttonwoods, The, H 1330
By Right of Conquest, H 570
Byles, M., character in Rebels, H 1185
Bynner, E. L., author of Agnes Surriage, H 1005
Begum's Daughter, H
Nimport, 98
Penelope's Suitors, H
Tritons, 387
Zachary Phipps, H 1835
Byrd, Col., character in His Great Self, H 982
Cabots, the, in Y. F.'s Amer. Explorers,
Cable, G: W., author of Bonaventure, 614
Dr. Sevier, H 2185
Grandissimes, 720
Madame Delphine, 808
Old Creole Days, 874
Strange True Stories, 964
Caecilia Metella, H190
Cahun, L., author of Captain Mago, H41
Calavar, H 545
Callista, H425
Cambyses, character in Daughter Egypt. King.
Camp Fires of Revo., H 1583
Canada, see Manitoba, New-Brunswick, Ontario, Quebec

INDEX.

Canadian Brothers, H 1915
Canadians of Old, H 1026
Canolles, H 1495
Cape-Breton, see Louisbourg
Capt. Kyd, H 950
Capt. Paul, H 1410
Capt. Phil, H 2235
Caracala, character in Thorny Path, H420
Carleton, H 1260
Carpenter, Edm. J., author of Woman of Shawmut, H
Carpenter, W: H., author Clairborne the Rebel, H Regicide's Daughter, H
Carruthers, W: A., author Cavaliers of Va., H 860
Carthage, scenes in Salammbo, H145
Cartier, character in Y. F.'s Amer. Explorers, H 590
Carver, Gov., character in Standish of Standish, H
Casimir Saral, H 1905
Cassiodorus, character in Struggle for Rome, H
Cassique, H 880
Castine, scene of Tales of the Puritans, Cat of Bubastes, H10
Catacombs described in Flora, H405
Catherwood, M., author Craque-O'-Doom, 221 Lady of Fort St. John, Rocky Fork, 126 Romance, H 807 Story of Tonty, H 885
Catlin, G:, author of Life Among the Indians, Catskills, scenes in Dutch Dominie, H 1385
Cavaliers of Va, H 860
Chainbearer, H 990
Champlain, char. in Y. F.'s Amer. Explorers,
Champlain, Lake, scene of Dutch Dominie, H 1385 Midshipman Paulding,
Champlin, J. F., author Y. F.'s Hist. Civil War,
Charicles, H135, 400
Charles, E. (R.), author of Lapsed, but not Lost, Victory of the Vanquished, H240
Charleston, scene of Bravo's Daughter, H Earth Trembled, H

Partisan, H 2195
Charlotte Temple, H 1510
Charlotte's Daughter, H 1511
Charmione, H115
Chateaubriand, author of Atala, H 610 Martyrs, H445
Cheney, C. E., author of Hist. Civil War, H 2295
Cheney, H. V., author of Peep at Pilgrims, H 740 Rivals of Acadia, H 745
Chesapeake Bay, scene of Within the Capes, H
Chesebro, Caroline, author Victoria, H 775
Chevalier, H., author of 39 men for one woman,
Chicago, scene of Waunangee, H 1925
Child, L. M., author of Hobomok, H 690 Philothea, H.190 Rebels, H 1185
Children of Destiny, H 2145
Christian Indian, H 645
Christian Rel., doctrin, in Cyllene, 470 Hypatia, H500 Christine, H 1275
Church, A. J., author of Pictures from Roman Life, H215 Three Greek Children. Two Thousand years ago, H170
Cicero, character in Two Thous. Years ago,
Cincinnati, scene of Wash Bolter, H 2120
Circuit-Rider, H 2082
Claiborne the Rebel, H 715
Clemens, J., author of Rivals, H 1805
Clement of Rome, H370
Cleopatra, H230, 235 Antonia, H495 Basil, 601 Dead Secret, 671
Clifford Family, H 1250
Cobb, Jo. B., author of Creoles, H 1855
Coligny, in Lily and the Totem, H
Collins, Wilkie, author of Evil Genius, 1255 Hide and Seek, 1359 Law and the Lady, 1461 No Name, 1619

Yellow Mask, 1023
Colonial Boy, H 630
Columbus, character in Heroes of Amer. Disc., Mercedes of Castile, H Y. F.'s Amer. Explorers, H 590
Connecticut, scene of Christian Indian, H 615 Dr. Johns, H. 1995 Fawn of Pale, H 725 Lost Hunter, H 730 Romance of Charter Oak Sketch of Conn., H 1508 Spectre of the Forest, H
Conspiracy of Burr, H 1825
Conspirator, H 1820
Constance Aylmer, H 820
Constance of Acadia, H 750
Constantine, Donation Struggle for Rome,
Conway, Gen. T:, char. in Quaker Soldier, H 1325
Cooke, J: E., author of Canolles, H 1495 Fairfax, H 1025 Hammer and Rapier, H Henry St. John, H 1215 Hilt to Hilt, H 2225 Justin Harley, H 1150 Last of the Foresters, H My Lady Pokahontas, Virginia Comedians, H Youth of Jefferson, H
Cooke, Rose (T.), author Steadfast, 143
Cooper, Ja. F., author of Deerslayer, H 1010 Jack Tier, H 2100 Last of Mohicans, H Lionel Lincoln, H 1230 Mercedes of Castile, H Miles Wallingford, H Pathfinder, H 1020 Pilot, H 1400 Pioneers, H 1010 Prairie, H 1658 Red Rover, H 1080 Satanstoe, H 990 Spy, H 1425 Water Witch, H 865 Wept of Wish-ton-wish, Wyandotte, H 1225
Coquette, H 1300
Corinth, character in Charicles, H135
Cornwallis, C. F., author Perikles, 104
Costal, H 1880
Council of Nikaia, in Arius, H465

INDEX.

Crawford, F.M., author of American Politician, 185
- Cigarette Maker, 643
- Dr. Claudius, 675
- Greifenstein, 724
- Marcio, 2595
- Mr. Isaacs, 843
- Paul Patoff, 894
- Roman Singer, 922, 2601
- Sant' Ilario, 933
- Saracinesca, 2602
- Tale of a lonely Parish, 1829
- To Leeward, 543
- Zoroaster, H65

Creasy, E. S., author of Old Love and the New, H130

Creole, H 1855
Crim, Mat., author of Adven. of a Fair Rebel,
Crockett, D:, character in Remember, H 2050
Croesus, character in Daughter of an Egyptian King, H80
Crown Jewels, H 2305
Cruising in the last war, H 1930
Cudjo's Cave, H 2200
Cushing, E. L., author of Saratoga, H 1295
Cyllene, H470

Dabney, V., author of Don Miff, H 2240
Dahn, Felix, author of Felicitas, H515
- Struggle for Rome, H520

Dall, C. (H), author of Romance of the Ass'n,
D'Auvers, N., author of Heroes of Amer. Disc.,
Darkness and Dawn, H325
Daughter of an Egyptian King, H80
David, character in Throne of David, H40
Davis, M. E. M., author In War Times, H 2245
Dawes, R., author of Nix Mate, H 890
Day in Ancient Rome, H195
Days of the Cocked Hats, H 900
Decatur and Somers, H 1800

Deerslayer, H 1010
De Forest, J: W:, author Honest John Vane, 270, Justine's Lovers, 284, H Miss Ravenel's Conversion, H 2220
- Playing Mischief, 342
- Seacliffe, 365
Delaware, scene of Koningsmarke, H 770
Delusion, H 930
Denison, M., author of Days of Cocked Hats, Master, 311
Derwent, H 1785
De Vere, M. S., author of Great Empress, H300
Dion and the Sibyls, H285
Dionysia, Feast of, in Charmione, H115
Disosway, T. T., author of South Meadows, H 940
Dr. Johns, H 1995
Dr. Le Baron, H 855
Dr. Sevier, H 2195
Don Miff, H 2240
Douglas, Marian, author Peter and Polly, H 1615
Down the Ohio, H 2140
Doyle, A. C., author of Refugees, H 883
Druids, described in Herminius, H315
Du Bois, C. G., author of Martha Corey, H 945
Duganne, A. J. H., author of Bravo's Daughter, H
Duke, S. R., author of Osceola, H 2055
Dumas, A, author of Capt. Paul, H 1410
Dupuy, E. A., author of Conspirator, H 1820
Dutch in America, in Constance Aylmer, H
First of Knickerbockers, Knickerbocker History,
Dutch Dominie, H 1385
Dutchman's Fireside, H 1027

Earle, A. (M.)
- Social Life in Old New Eng., H 1655
Earth Trembled, H 2315
Ebers, G., author of Bride of the Nile, H505
- Cleopatra, H235
- Dau. Egyptian King.
- Emperor, H390
- Homo Sum, H460

Joshua, H20
Margery, 820
Question, H99
Serapis, H485
Sisters, H1155
Thorny Path, H420
Uarda, H30
Eckstein, E., author of Aphrodite, H90
- Nero, H320
- Prusias, H165
- Quintus Claudius,
- Will, the, 1018
Edge Hill, H 1525
Edith, H 780
Edwards, Pierpont, char. Coquette, H 1300
Old Town Folks, H
Edwin Brothertoft, H 1610
Eggleston, E:, author of Circuit Rider, 15, H
- Graysons, 40, H 2070
- Hoosier School Master, 52, H 2080
- Montezuma, H 575
- Roxy, 131, H 2084
Eggleston, G: C., author Man of Honor, 79
- Red Eagle, H 1895
Egypt, manners in Life of Herodotus, H95
Egyptian,
- Azeth the Egyptian, H55
Eighteen hundred forty-four, H 2000
Elkswatawa, H 1885
Emperor, H390
Empress, H295
End of the World, H 2086
Endicott, Gov., char. in Merry Mount, H 685
English, T: D., author of 1844, H 2000
- Jacob Schuyler's Millions, 759
Englishman's Haven, H 1013
Foneguski, H 1890
Epicurean, H435
Escrich, E. P., author of Martyr of Golgotha, H265
Ethan Allen, H 1245
Euripides, character in Aspasia, H1110
Evangeline, H 1030
Evans, A. J., author of Inez, H 2045
- St. Elmo, 931

4

Explorers,
  Heroes of Amer. Discovery, H 595
  Y. F.'s Book of Amer. Explorers, H 590
Eyster, Nellie, author of Colonial Boy, H 630
Ezra, character in King of Tyre, H85
Fabiola, H450
Fair God, H 565
Fairfax, H 1025
Fair Puritan, H 895
Fair to Look Upon, H44
Family without a name, H 2085
Farrar, F: W:, author of Darkness and Dawn,
Fatal Marriage, H 1145
Fawn of Pale faces, H 725
Fawn of Sertorius, H1160
Feast of Dionysia, in Charmione, H115
Felicitas, H515
Ferry, Gabriel, author of Costal, H 1880
First of the Knickerbockers, H 805
Five Hundred Majority, H 2310
Flamingo Feather, H 620
Flaubert, G., author of Madame Bovary, 2122
  Salammbo 932, H1145
Flora, H405
Florian, author of Numa Pompilius, H57
Florida, scene of
  Flamingo Feather, H
  Jack Tier, H 2100
  Lily and the Totem, H
  Vasconselos, H 600
For the Temple, H340
Forest Tragedy, H 1375
Forsaken, H 1515
Fosdick, W: W., author Malmitzic, H 560
Foster, H., author of Coquette, H 1300
FRAETAS, I. A., author Ethan Allen, H 1245
France, A., author of Thais, H280
Frankland, H:, char. in Agnes Surriage, H 1060
Franklin, character in Israel Potter, H 1415
  Thro' Colonial Doorways
Frederick de Algeroy, H 1455
Frederic, Harold, author

in the Valley, H 1395
Frederic, Md., scene of Colonial Boy, H 630
Freeney, Belle, author of Fair to Look Upon H44
French, D. C., author of Elkswatawa, H 1885
Gallus, H225-400
Garret van Horn, H 2095
Gaspe, author of Canadians of Old, H
Gautier, Theo., author Romance of a Mummy.
George Balcomb, H 1700
George Stalden, H 1115
Georgia, scene of
  Lily and the Totem, H
  On a Plantation, H 2280
Geraldine Hawthorne, H 1620
Gilbert, H., character in Amer. Explorers, H 590
Gilman, A., author of Story of Rome, H58
Gladiator, H410
Gladiators, The, H335
Gladiators (see Amphitheatre), revolt of, in Prasias, H165
Two Thousand years ago, H175
Goffe, character in Mt. Hope, H 840
  Romance of Charter Oak Tales of Puritans, H
  Three Judges, H 845
Golden Age
  Story of Golden Age,
Gomery of Montgomery, H 1870
Gordon, W: J., author of Englishman's Haven, H
Gore, Cath. G., author Agathonia, H 525
Goss, W. L., author of Jed, H 2255
Goths, described in
  Antonina, H495
  Attila, H510
  House of the Wolfings, Struggle for Rome.
Gourges, D. de, char. in Lily and the Totem, H
Grace Dudley, H 1290
Graham, J: W., author of Neaera, H290
Grandfather's Chair, H 675, H 695
Grant, A (M.), author of

Memoirs of Amer. Lady, H 1090
Grayson, E., author of Overing, H 1595
  Standish the Puritan, H
Graysons, H 2070
Great Empress, H300
Great Treason, H 1625
Greece, history, futility of novels of, H58
Greece, manners in
  Athenian Letters, H120
  Charicles, H135
  Life of Herodotus, H95
Greeley, Ro. F., author of Old Cro Nest, H 1125
Green Mt. Boys, H 1170
Greenough, H., author of Apelles, H140
Greenwood, G., author of Forest Tragedy, H 1375
Grey Hawk, H 1950
Greyslaer, H 1360
Guert Ten Eyck, H 1630
Hagar, character in Fair to Look Upon, H44
Haggard, H: R., author Cleopatra, H230
  Jess, 764
  Montezuma's Daughter, She, 939
Hale, E. E., author of
  If, Yes, and Perhaps, 746
  Man Without a Country, 815
  Mr. Tangier's Vacation, 318
  Philip Nolan, H 1780
  Ups and Downs, 395
Hale, Nathan, char. in Guert Ten Eyck, H
Hall, C. W., author of Twice Taken, H 1015
Hall, J. A., author of Legends of West, H
Hamerling, Ro., author Aspasia, H110
Hamilton, A., char. in Guert Ten Eyck, H
  Loyal Little Redcoat, H
Hamilton, J., author of Philo, H275
Hammer and Rapier, H 2230
Handwriting on the Wall, H70
Hannibal, character in Salammbo, H145

5

INDEX.

Hansford, H 870
Hardwicke, author,
  Athenian Letters, H120
Harland, M., author of
  Alone, 2 9
  Gallant Fight, H 257
  His Great Self, H 982
  Jessamine, H 278
  Judith, H 2025
Harper, F., author of
  Iola Leroy, H 2155
Harrington, H 2105
Harris, J. C., author
  Free Joe, 708
  On a Plantation, H 2280
Harris, M (C.), author of
  Phoebe, 340
  Sutherlands, H 1140
Harry Burnham, H 1580
Hart and His Bear, H 2620
Haunted Wood, H 1315
Haverhill, H 1070
Hawks of Hawk Hollow, H 1528
Hawthorne, N., author of
  Blitheday Romance, 610
  Grandfather's Chair, H 695
  House of Seven Gables, 743
  Marble Fawn, 817
  Scarlet Letter, H 795
  True Stories, H 675
  Twice Told Tales, H 660
Heath, Ja. E., author of
  Edge Hill, H 1525
Hebrew Tales, H180
Hellas,
  Pictures of Hellas, H3
Helon's Pilgrimage, H158
Henry St. John, H 1215
Henty, G: A., author of
  By Right of Conquest, H 570
  Cat of Bubastes, H10
  For the Temple, H340
  With Lee, H 2260
  With Wolfe, H 1065
  Young Carthagenian,
Hentz, N: M., author of
  Tadenskund, H 1048
Herbert, H: W.,author of
  Fair Puritan, H 895
  Roman Traitor, H175
Herbert Wendall, H 1530
Herminius, H315
Herod the Great, H185
Herodotus,
  Boys' and Girls' H—, 97

Life & Trav. of Herodotus, H95
Heroes of American Discovery, H 595
Herr, A. J., author of
  Maid of the Valley, H
Hetairai, described in Charicles, H135
Higginson, T: W., author
  Amer. Explorers, H 590
  Malbone, 78
Hilt to Hilt, H 2225
Hiram, King, char. in
  King of Tyre, H185
His Great Self, H 982
Hobomok, H 690
Hoffman, C: F., author of
  Greyslaer, H 1630
Holland, J. G., author of
  Arthur Bonnycastle, 191
  Bay Path, H 602
  Miss Gilbert's Career,86
Hollister, G. H., author of
  Mt. Hope, H 840
Homes of America, H 1200
Homo Sum, H460
Honest John Vane, H 2285
Hoosier School Master, H 2080
Hope, A. J., author of
  Men of the Backwoods,
Hope Leslie, H 790
Hopkins, S:, author of
  Youth of the Old Dominion, H 625
Hoppus, M. A., author of
  Great Treason, H 1625
Horace, character in
  Pictures from Roman Life, H215
Horseshoe Robinson, H 1485
Hot Ploughshares, H 2130
House of the Wolfings, H475
Houston, S:, character in
  Remember, H 2045
Hudson's Bay Co., in
  Snow Shoes, H 1955
Huguenots, in
  Flamingo Feather, H
  Lily and the Totem, H
  Rivals, H 1805
Hundred Boston Orators, H 1640
Hypatia, H500
Illinois, scene of
  Zury, H 1970
  In the Boyhood of Lincoln, H 1985

In Leisler's Times, H 905
In Old Quinnebasset, H 1790
In Old Virginia, H 2150
In the Valley, H 1395
In War Times, H 2245
Indiana, scene of
  Circuit-Rider, H 2082
  End of the World, H
  Hoosier Schoolmaster,
  Roxy, H 2084
Indians, see Redmen
Inez, H 2045
Infidel, H 550
Ingraham, J. H., author
  Burton, H 1255
  Capt. Kyd, H 950
  Lafitte, H 1845
  Pillar of Fire, H15
  Prince of the House of David, H260
  Quadroon, H 1095
  South West, H 1685
  Throne of David, H40
Insurgents, The, H 1760
Iola Leroy, H 2155
Irving, W., author of
  Knickerbocker History,
Israel Potter, H 1415
Issachar,
  Son of Issachar, H257
Jack Horner, H 2265
Jack Tier, H 2100
Jackson, Andrew, char. in
  Eoneguski, H 1890
Jackson, G: A., author of
  Son of a Prophet, H45
Jackson, "Stonewall,"
  Old Jack, H 2205
Jamaica, scene of
  Haverhill, H 1070
James, G: P. R., author
  Adrian, H 1735
  Attila, H510
  Old Dominion, H 2035
  String of Pearls, 967
  Ticonderoga, H 1035
Jed, H 2255
Jefferson, T:, char. in
  Youth of Jefferson, H
Jesus, character in
  Ben Hur, H250
  Julian, H270
  Martyr of Golgotha,
  Philochristus, H253
  Prince of House of David,
  Son of Issachar, H257
Jerusalem, siege
  For the Temple, H340
  Gladiators, H335
  Naomi, H345

Jews, manners of, in
   Life of Herodotus, H95
John Godfrey's Fortunes,
   H 2175
Johnson, Sir W:, char. in
   M., Derwent, H 1380
Johnson Manor, H 1155
Jones, Ja. A., author of
   Haverhill. H 1070
Jones, J: R,
   Monarchist, H 1585
   Quaker Soldier, H 1325
Jones, N. J., author of
   Simon Girty, H 975
Jones, Paul, char. in
   Israel Potter, H 1415
   Pilot, H 1460
Josephus.
   Our Young Folks' Josephus, H1245
Joshua, H20
Journal of a Young Lady,
   H 1755
Judith, H 2025
Julia of Baiae, H330
Julian, H270
Julian, Emperor, char. in
   Julian, H270
   Last Athenian, H455
   Parthenia, H480
Justin Harley, H 1150
Justine's Lovers, H 2290
Justinian, character in
   Struggle for Rome,
   H520

Kabaosa, H 1920
Kate Aylesford, H 1280
Katherine Walton, H 1475
Kennedy, J: P., author of
   Horseshoe Robinson, H
   Rob of the Bowl, H
   Swallow Barn, H 2005
Kent, Ja., author of
   Johnson Manor, H 1155
   Sibyl Spencer, H 942
Kentucky, scene of
   Beauchampe, H 1710
   Boone, H 1720
   Lonz Powers, H 1715
   Men of the Backwoods,
   Nick of the Woods, H
   Uncle Tom's Cabin, H
   2010
   Westward Ho! H 1695
Keon, M. G., author of
   Dion & the Sibyls,
King of the Hurons, H
   970
King of Tyre, H113
King's Treasure House,
   H27

Kingsley, C:, author of
   Hypatia, H500
Kingston, W: H. G., author of
   Snow Shoes, H 1955
Kinsmen, H 1470
Kip, L., author of
   Aenone, H380
   Dead Marquise, 670
   Nestlenook, 861
Kirke, E., author of
   My Southern Friends,
Kirkland, C. M. F.
   Life of Washington, H
   1645
Kirkland, Jo., author of
   McVeys, H 1975
   Zury, H 1970
Knickerbocker Hist. of
   New York, H 1650
Knight, Cor., author of
   Marcus Flaminius, H283
Knight of the Golden
   Mellice, H 710
Knights of the Horse
   Shoe, H 980
Koningsmarke, H 770
Konns, N. C., author of
   Arius the Libyan, H465
Labree, L., author of
   Rebels and Tories, H
   1370
Lady of Fort St. John,
   H 750
Lafitte, H 1845, H 1850
Laing, Caroline (Butler)
   Seven Kings, H58
Lamb, M. J., author of
   Homes of America, H
   1200
Lamont, M. M., author of
   Gladiator, H410
Landor, W. S., author of
   Perikles & Aspasia,
   H110
Lapsed but not Lost,
   H430
La Salle, character in
   Story of Tonty, H 855
Last Athenian, H455
Last Days of Pompeii,
   H350
Last of the Foresters, H
   1135
Last of the Mohicans, H
   1017
La Tour, character in
   Rivals, H 1805
Laudonniere, character in
   Flamingo Feather, H
   Amer. Explorers, H 590

Lawrence, E., author of
   George Stalden, H. H15
Lea, H375
Leatham, E. A., author
   Charmione, H115
Leather Stocking and Silk,
Leaves from Ma. Smith's
   Journal, H 875
Lee, E. (B.), author of
   Delusion, H 930
   Naomi, H 790
   Parthenia, H480
Legends of the West, H
   1860
Leister, character in
   Begum's Daughter, H
   Leister's Times. H 905
Le Sage, author of
   Bachelor of Salamanca,
Letters from Palmyra,
   H440
Lexington, scene of
   Lionel Lincoln, H 1230
Life Among the Indians,
   H 1900
Life of Herodotus, H95
Lily and the Totem, H
   615
Lincoln, A., character in
   Boyhood of Lincoln, H
   Azeth the Egyptian,
   H55
   Patricia Kemball, 1666
   Through the Long
   Nights, 1850
Linwoods, H 1533
Lionel Lincoln, H 1230
Lippard, G., author of
   Blanche of Brandywine, H 1285
   Paul Ardenheim, H
   Quaker City, 350
   Rose of Wissahickon, H
Littlepage Manuscripts, in
   Satanstoe, H 990
Lockhart, J. G., author
   Valerius, H365
Lockwood, R., author of
   Insurgents, H 1760
Lone Dove, H 1297
Longfellow, H: W., author of
   Evangeline, H 1030
   Kavanagh, 66
Longinus, character in,
   Zenobia, H440
Long Island, scene of
   Christine, H 1275
   Van Gelder, H 1160
Lonz Powers, H 1750

7

INDEX.

Loring, J. S.
  Hundred Boston Orators, H 1640
Lost Hunter, H 730
Louisbourg, scenes of
  Englishman's Haven, H
  Twice Taken, H 1015
Louisiana, scene of
  Harrington, H 2105
  Philip Nolan, H 1780
Lovers' Trials, H 901
Loyal Little Redcoat, H750
Ludlow, J. M., author of
  King of Tyre, 113
Lummis, C: F., author of
  Spanish Pioneers, H 585
Lytton, baron, author of
  Disowned, 674
  Ernest Maltravers, 685
  Kenelm Chillingly, 1427
  Last Days of Pompeii, H350
  Pausanias, H85
  Parisians, the, 889
  Pelham, 896m
  Strange Story, 963

Maccabees, characters in Helon's Pilgrimage.
McHenry, Ja., author of
  Spectre of the Forest, H Wilderness, H 1035
McKnight, C:, author of
  Old Ft. Duquesne, H
McVeys, H 1975
Maecenas, character in
  Pictures from Roman Life, 215
Magicians,
  Master of the Magicians, 60
Maid of the Valley, H 1365
Maine, scene of
  Agamenticus, H 1085
  In Old Quinnebasset, H
Malachi, character in
  King of Tyre, 85
Malmitzic, H 560
Man Without a Country, H 1830
Manitoba, scene of
  Grey Hawk, H 1950
Marcus Aurelius, char. in Marius, 400
Marcus Flaminius, 283
Margaret Mongrieff, H 1273
Mariager, Peder, author
  Pictures of Hellas, H3
Marion and his Men, H 1445

Marion's Brigade, H 1450
Marius the Epicurean, H400
Markham, R:, author of
  King Philip's War, H
Marksman of Monmouth, H 1335
Marrying by Lot, H 1740
Martha Corey, H 945
Martial, character in
  Pictures from Roman Life, H215
Martyr of Golgotha, H265
Martyrs, H445
Martyrs of Carthage, H415
Mary Derwent, H 1380
Mary Magdalene, char.
  Martyr of Golgotha, H265
Maryland, scene of
  Claiborne, H 715
  Fatal Marriage, H 1145
  Rob of the Bowl, H 813
Massachusetts, scene of
  Bay Path, H 705
  Hope Leslie, H 700
  Leaves fr. Ma. Smith's journal, H 875
  Linwoods, H 1535
  Merry Mount, H 685
  More Good Times, H
  Mt. Hope, H 840
  Qualbhin, H 2000
  Scarlet Letter, H 795
  True Stories, H 675
  Twicetold Tales, H 660
  —see Boston, Plymouth, Salem
Massasoit, char. in
  Peep at Pilgrims, H 740
Master of the Magicians, H60
Master of Tanagra, H127
Mather, I., char. in
  Romance of Charter Oak, H 843
Mathews, C., author of
  Behemoth, H 530
  Chanticleer, H 209
Matilda Montgomerie, H 1916
Maturin, E., author of
  Montezuma, H 555
  Sejanus, H305
May Martin, H 1730
May, Sophie, author of
  Drone's Honey, 237
  In old Quinnebasset, H
Mellichampe, H 1465
Melville, G: J: W., author of

Gladiators, H335
Rosine, 928
Sarchedon, H50
Melville, H., author of
  Israel Potter, H 1415
Memorials of So. Planter, H 2300
Memphis, scenes in
  Sisters, H155
Men of the Backwoods, H 1680
Mercedes of Castile, H 540
Meridith, H 1320
Merry Mount, H 685
Meschinza, described in
  Meridith, H 1320
Mexico, scene of
  Bachelor of Salamanca, Costal, H 1880
  Crown Jewels, H 2305
  Montezuma, H 555
  Queen of Savannah, H
Meyers, P: H., author of
  First of Knickerbockers,
  King of the Hurons, H
  Prisoner, H 2060
  Young Patroon, H 915
Midshipman Paulding, H 1945
Miles Wallingford, H 1770
Miletus, scenes in
  Aphrodite, H90
Minister's Wooing, H 1175
Minnesota, scene of
  Mystery of Metropolisville, H 2180
  Tales of North West, H 1675
Mirage of Promise, H 2015
Miss Ravenel's Conversion, H 2220
Missing Bride, H 1935
Mitchell, D. G., author of
  Dr. Johns, H 1995
Modern Chivalry, H 1765
Moffett, E. L., author of
  Crown Jewels, H 2305
Mohawk Valley, scene of
  Forest Tragedy, H 1375
  Greyslaer, H 1360
  In the Valley, H 1395
  Mary Derwent, H 1380
  Paul and Persis, H 1390
  Rebels and Tories, H
Monarchist, H 1585
Monnier, M:, author of
  Pompeii, H355

Montezuma, char. in
  By Right of Conquest, H
  Calavar, H 545
  Fair God, H 565
  Infidel, H 550
  Malmitzic, H 560

INDEX.

Montezuma, H 375
Montezuma's Daughter,
Montezuma's Dinner, H
Moore, T:, author of
 Epicurean, H435
Moravians, in
 Marrying by Lot, H
 Victorious Defeat, H
More Good Times, H 2075
Morford, H:, author of
 Spur of Monmouth, H
Morgan, L: H., author of
 Montezuma's Dinner, H
Mormonism, in
 Buttons Inn, H 2030
Morris, W:, author of
 House of the Wolfings,
Mortimer, C., author of
 Marrying by Lot, H
Morton's Hope, H 1540
Moses, character in
 Cat of Bubastes, H10
 Pillar of Fire, H15
Motley, J: L., author of
 Merry Mount, H 685
 Morton's Hope, H 1540
Mound-Builders, in
 Behemoth, H 530
 Children's Stories, H
Mt. Hope, H 840
Mt. Vernon, scene of
 Colonial Boy, H 630
Mummy,
 Romance of a M—,
Munro, K., author of
 Flamingo Feather, H
Murdock, D:, author of
 Dutch Dominie, H 1385
Murgatroyd, M., author of
 Refugee, H 1500
My Lady Pocahontas, H 635
My Southern Friends, H 2110
Myrtle, A. T., author of
 Ambrosio, H 2040
Mysteries of the People, H247
Nameless Noblemen, H765
Naomi, H345
Naomi, H 790
Nenera, H290
Neal, J:, author of
 True Womanhood, H 1345
Near to Nature's Heart, H 1345
Nebuchadnezzar, char.
 Master of the Magicians, H60
Nehemiah, character in
 King of Tyre, H85
Neighbor Jackwood, H 2065
Nero, H320

Nero, character in
 Darkness & Dawn,
 Empress, H295
 Great Empress, H300
 Sejanus, H305
New Brunswick, scene of
 Constance, H 755
 Lady of Fort, H 750
 Rivals, H 745
New-Jersey, scene of
 Star and the Cloud, H
New-London, scene of
 Old Harbor Town, H
Newman, J: H:, author of
 Callista, H425
New-Orleans, scene of
 Dr. Sevier, H 2185
 Quadroon, H 1095
Newport, scene of
 Minister's Wooing, H
 Red Rover, H 1080
New-York (city), scene of
 Begum's Daughter, H
 Charlotte Temple, H
 Constance, H 820
 First of Knickerbockers,
 Five Hundred Majority,
 In Leisler's Time, H 905
 King of the Hurons, H
 Knickerbocker's hist., H
 Loyal Little Redcoat, H
 Sutherlands, H 1140
 True Womanhood, H
 Young Patroon, H 915
New-York (state), (see also
 Catskills, Long-Island,
 Mohawk), scene of
 Deerslayer, H 1010
 Dutchman's Fireside, H
 Grace Dudley, H 1290
 Johnson Manor, H 2175
 Last of Mohicans, H
 Linwoods, H 1535
 Old Crow Nest, H 1125
 Pathfinder, H 1020
 Saltillo Boys, H 2125
 Saratoga, H 1050
 Spy, H 1425
 Ticonderoga, H 1055
 Van Gelder, H 1160
 Wyandotte, H 1225
Nick of Woods, H 1705
Nile,
 Bride of the Nile, H505
 Priest of the Nile, H26
Niles, Wyllis, author of
 500 majority, H 2310
Nix' Mate, H 890
Numa Pompilius, H 57
O'Connor, W:, author of
 Harrington, H 2105
Ogden, Ruth, author of
 Loyal Little Redcoat, H
Ohio, scene of
 Ansel's Cave, H 1960

Down the Ohio, H 2140
Hart, H 2020
Rocky Fork, H 126
Old Continental, H 1555
Old Crow Nest, H 1125
Old Dominion, H 2035
Old Fort Duquesne, H
Old Hicks the Guide, H 1725
Old Jack, H 2205
Old Love and the New, H130
Old Town Stories, H 1305
Olympia, H75
On Newfound River, H 2135
On a Plantation, H 2230
Ontario, scene of
 Algonquin, H 1075
 Family Without a Name,
 Prisoner of Border, H
 Refugees, H 1500
 Romance, H 807
 Story of Tonty, H 885
Orlando Chester, H 1130
Osceola, H 2055
Our Young Folks' Josephus, H247
Overing, H 1595
Page, T: N., author of
 Among the Camps, H
 In Ole Virginia, 749, H
 On Newfound River, H
 Two Little Confederates, H 2250
Palmyra, described in
 Zenobia, H440
Pancratius, St., char. in
 Fabiola, H450
Parker, H.. F., author of
 Constance Aylmer, H 1480
Parthenia, H480
Partisan, H 1435
Partisan Leader, H 2195
Pater, W., author of
 Marius, H400
Pathfinder, H 1020
Paul and Persis, H 1390
Paul Ardenheim, H 1560
Paul Jones, H 1405, H 1410, H 1420
Paulding, J. K., author of
 Dutchman's Fireside, H
 Koningsmarke, H 770
 Old Continental, H 1555
 Puritan and His Daughter, H 810
 Westward Ho! H 1695
Pausanias, H85
Peculiar, H 2115
Peep at Pilgrims, H 740
Pelasgi, history, in
 Pictures of Hellas, H3

9

Pemberton, H 1460
Penelope's Suitors, H 995
Pennsylvania, scene of
  Blanche, H 1285
  Hawks, H 1520
  Marrying by Lot,H 1740
  Modern Chivalry, H
  Old Fort Duquesne, H
  Paul Ardenheim, H 1560
  Quaker Soldier, H 1325
  Rose of Wis., H 1265
  Simon Girty, H 975
  Story of Kennett, H
  Wilderness, H 1035
Perikles, H104
Perikles, character in
  Amymone, H105
  Aspasia, H110
  Athenian Letters,H120
  Charmione, H115
  Philothea, H100
Persia, manners, in
  Life of Herodotus,H95
Peter and Polly, H 1615
Peterson, C. J., author of
  Cruising in the Last War, H 1930
  Grace Dudley, H 1290
  Kate Aylesford, H 1280
  Pemberton, H 1460
Pheidias, character in
  Aspasia, H110
Phelps, E. S., author of
  Master of the Magicians, H60
Philadelphia, scene of
  Forsaken, H 1515
  Meredith, H 1320
  Colonial Doorways, H 1665
Philip, King, char. in
  King Philip's War, 850
  Mt. Hope, H 840
  Peep at Pilgrims, H 740
Philip Nolan, H 1780
Philo, H275
Philochristus, H253
Philosophy, ancient, des.
  Last Athenian, H455
  Marius, H400
  Philo, H275
Philothea, H100
Phryne, char. in
  Master of Tanagra
Pictures from Roman Life, H215
Pictures of Hellas, H3
Pictures of Olden Time, H 665
Pike, M., author of
  Agnes, H 1600

Berenice,Gr.
Pillar of Fire, H15
Pilot, H 1400
Pioneer Women, H 1875
Pioneers, The, H 1010
Pirates, in
  Capt. Kyd, H 950
  Lafitte, H 1845
  Ramon, H 955
  Treasure Island, H 965
Pittsburg, scene of
  Old Ft. Duquesne, H
Plato, character in
  Charmione, H113
  Philothea, H100
Pliny, character in
  Pictures from Roman Life, H215
Plutarch,
  Boys' and Girls' Plutarch
Plymouth, scenes of
  Betty Alden, H 735
  Dr. Le Baron, H 855
  Hobomok, H 690
  Nameless Nobleman, H
  Peep at Pilgrims, H 740
  Pictures, H 665
  Standish of Standish, H
Pocahontas, character in
  Children's Stories,H 535
  Life of Smith, H 640
  My Lady Pocahontas, H 635
  Pocahontas,
Pompeii, H355
Pompeii,
  Last Days of Pompeii, H
Pompey, character in
  Fawn of Sertorius,
Poore, B. P., author of
  Scout, H 1575
Prairie, H 1658
Price of Peace, H47
Priest of the Nile, H26
Prince of the House of David, H260
Prisoner of the Border, H 2060
Prolus, 441
Prusias, H165
Puritan and his Daughter, H 810
Puritan and Quaker, H 800
Pyle, H., author of
  Within the Capes, H
Pythagoras, char. in
  Daughter of Egypt, King, H80
Quabbin, H 2000

Quadroon, H 984
Quaker Soldier, H 1325
Quakers, in
  Down the Ohio, H 2140
Quakers, persecution of in
  Edith, H 780
  Ma. Smith, H 875
  Naomi, H 790
  Puritan and Quaker, H
Quebec, scene of
  Brandon, H 1060
  Burton, H 1255
  Canadians of Old, H
  Haverhill, H 1070
  With Wolfe, H 1065
Queen of the Savanna, H 1990
Quintus Claudius, H360
Rachel, character in
  Fair to Look Upon,
Rachel Stanwood, H 2160
Rameses, H25
Rameses II., character
  Priest of the Nile, H26
  Rameses, H25
  Uarda, H30
Ramon, H 995
Rangers, H 1240
Raphael,Ben Isaac,H255
Ravenna, described in
  Antonina, H495
Rebels, H 1185
Rebels and Tories, H 1370
Red Eagle, H 1895
Redmen described in
  Life Among the Indians,
  Creeks in Atala, H 610
  Red Eagle, H 1895
  Iroquois in Romance, H 807
  Mohicans in Last of Mohicans, H 1047
  Ottawa in Greyhawk, H
  Pequods in Peep at Pilgrims,
  Seminoles in Atala, H 610; Osceola, H 2055
  Sioux in Prairie, H 1658
Red Revenger, H 960
Red Rover, H 1080
Refugees, H 883
Regicide's Daughter, H 841
Rejected Wife, H 1180
Remember the Alamo, H 2050
Reynolds, B. A., author
  Casimir Saral, H 1904
Rhode Island, scene of
  Minister's Wooing, H
  Mount Hope, H 840
  Oreeing, H 1595
Rhodes, scenes, in
  Agathonia, H525

INDEX.

Richard Hurdis, H 1690
Richardson, B: W., author of Son of a Star, H395
Richardson, J:, author of Canadian Brothers.
Richmond, scene of Jack Horner, H 2265
Riddle, A. G., author of Alice Brand, 183
Hart, H 2020
Ansel's Cave, H 1960
Rivals, H 1805
Rivals of Acadia, H 745
Rob of the Bowl, H 813
Roberts, C: H., author of Down the Ohio, H 2140
Robinson, J: H., author of Marion's Brigade, H
Rocky Mts., scene of Heroes, H 595
Roe, A. S., author of James Mountjoy, 61f
Like and Unlike, 71v.
Long Look Ahead, 71m.
Star and the Cloud, H
Roe, E: P., author of Earth Trembled, H
Near to Nature's Heart,
Young Girl's Wooing, 0412
Roman Nights, H205
Roman Traitor, H175
Romance of a Mummy, 115
Romance of Dollard, H 807
Romance of the Association, H 1310
Romance of the Charter Oak, H 843
Romance of the Revolution H 1655
Rome,
Day in Ancient Rome,
Story of ———, 1158
Struggle for Rome.
Visit to Ancient Rome.
Rose of Wissahikon, H 1265
Rowson, H., author of Charlotte Temple, H
Roxy, H 2084
Royalist's Daughter, H 1386
Rydberg, V:, author of Last Athenian, H455
Sackett's Harbor, scene of Midshipman.
Salammbo, H145
Salem, scene of Hobomok, H 690
House of Seven Gables,
Martha Corey, H 945
Salem Witchcraft, H
Two Hundred Years

Ago, H 785
Salem Belle, H 935
Salem Witchcraft, H 920
Saltillo Boys, H 2125
Saratoga, H 1050, H 1205
Sarchedon, H50
Sargent, E., author of Peculiar, H 2115
Sassacus, char. in Peep at Pilgrims, H 740
Satanstoe, H 990
Sauzade, J. S., author of Garret van Horn, H 2095
Scarlet Letter, H 795
Scenes in Washington, H 1840
Scipio, character in Sisters, H155
Scout, H 1171, H 1575
Scudder, H., author of Washington, 1645
Sealsfield, C:, author of Life in the New World.
Tokeah, H 1660
Sears, E. H., author of Pictures of Olden Times.
Seawell, M. E., author of Children of Destiny, H
Decatur and Somers, H
Midshipman Paulding, H
Paul Jones, H 1420
Sebastian, St., character Fabiola, H450
Sedgwick, C. M., author Hope Leslie, H 700
Linwoods, H 1535
Travelers, H 1980
Sejanus, H305
Sejanus, character in Dion, H285
Semiramis, character in Sarchedon, H50
Serapis, H485
Sertorius.
Fawn of Sertorius.
Seton, W:, author of Romance of Charter Oak, H 843
Seven Kings, H58
Shay's Rebellion in Insurgents, H 1760
Shumway, E. S., author Day in Ancient Rome.
Sigourney, L. (H.) Lucy Howard's Journal, 778
Sketch of Conn., 1508
Simeon Styntes, St., char. in Last Athenian, H455
Simms, W: G., author of Beauchampe, H 1710
Cassique, H 880

Kath. Walton, H 1475
Kinsman, H 1470
Lily and the Totem, H
Mellichampe, H 1465
Partisan, H 1435
Richard Hurdis, H 1690
Sword and Distaff, H
Vasconselos, H 600
Yemassee, H 983
Simon Girty, M 975
Simon Kenton, H 1590
Sisters, the, H155
Sketch of Conn., H 1508
Slave, the, H210
Slavery, described in Harrington, H 2120
Hot Ploughshares, H
Iola, H 2155
Mirage of Promise, H
My Southern Friends, H
Peculiar, H 2115
Uncle Tom's Cabin, H
Smith, E. O., author of Western Captive, H 1665
Smith, Horace, author of Tales of the Early Ages, H220
Smith, J: character in Pocahontas, H 635
Christian Indian, H 645
Life of, H 640
Amer. Explorers, H 590
Smith, M: P., author of Browns, 204
Great Match, 42
Jolly Good Times, 64
More Good Times, H
Smith, R: P., author of Forsaken, H 1515
Snelling, Anna, author of Kabaosa, H 1920
Snelling, W:, author of Tales of the Northwest,
Sneyd, H:, author of Cyllene, H470
Sneyd, Honora, char. in Pemberton, H 1490
Snow Shoes, H 1955
Social Life in Old N. E., H 1655
Socrates, character in Aspasia, H110
Charmione, H115
Solomon, character in Son of a Prophet, H45
Son of Issachar, H257
Son of a Prophet, H45
Son of a Star, H395
Sophokles, character in Aspasia, H110
Charmione, H115

11

INDEX.

Soto, H. de, char. in
  Heroes, H 595
  Life of, H 605
  Vasconselos, H 600
  Y, F's Amer. Explorers,
    H 880
South-Carolina, scenes of
  Cassique, H 880
  Horse Shoe Robinson, H 1485
  Kath Walton, H 1475
  Kinsman, H 1470
  Lily and the Totem, H 615
  Mellichampe, H 1465
  Miss Ravenel's Conversion, H 2220
  Swamp Steed, H 1490
  Yemassee, H 983
South Meadows, H 940
Southwest, The, H 1685
Southworth, E. D. E. N., author of
  Fatal Marriage, H 1145
  Missing Bride, H 1935
Souvestre, E., author of
  Attic Philosopher, 1962
  Brittany & La Vendee, 1974
  Leaves from a family journal, 2099
  Man and Money, 2041
  Slave, H210
  Visit to Ancient Rome, Workman's Confession, 2314
Spanish Pioneers, H 585
Sparta, life in
  Olympia, H75
Spectre of the Forest, H 827
Spur of Monmouth, H 1340
Spy, H 1425
Standish, Miles, char. in
  Betty Alden, H 735
  Merry Mount, H 685
  Peep at Pilgrims, H 740
Standish of Standish, H 670
Standish the Puritan, H 1570
Star and the Cloud, H 1165
Steadfast, 143
Stephens, A. S., author of
  Mary Derwent, H 1380
  Rejected Wife, H 1180
Stevenson, Ro. L., author
  Master of Ballantrae, 834
  Prince Otto, 901
  Treasure Island, H 965

Stoddard, W: O., author
  Among the Lakes, 3
  Guert Ten Eyck, H
  Saltillo Boys, H 2125
  Winter Fun, 173b
Stories of Persons, H 1205
Story of Kennett, H 1775
Story of Rome, H58
Story of the Golden Age, H35
Story of Tonty, H 885
Stowe, H. (B.), author of
  Dred, 678
  Little Pussy Willow, 294
  Minister's Wooing, 840,
  My Wife and I, 323
  Oldtown Fireside Stories, 107
  Old Town Folks, 106,
  Pearl of Orr's Island, 113
  Pink and White Tyranny, 341
  Uncle Tom's Cabin, H
  We and our Neighbors, 400
Strauss, F:, author of
  Helon's Pilgrimage, Lea, H375
Strickland, A., author of
  Alda, H310
Struggle for Rome, H520
Sue, Eugene, author
  Mysteries of the People
Suicide, described in
  Gallus, H225
Sutherlands, H 1140
Swallow Barn, H 2005
Swamp Steed, H 1490
Swedes in Amer., in
  Koningsmarke, H 770
Sword and Distaff, H 1480
Tadenskund, H 1048
Tales of the Early Ages, H220
Tales of the Northwest,
Tales of the Puritans, H 825
Tales of the Times, H 655
Tanagra, Master of Tanagra, 127
Tanner, J:, author of
  Grey Hawk, H 1950
Taylor, Bayard, author of
  Beauty and the Beast, 6
  J: Godfrey, 280
  Joseph and His Friend, 65
  Hannah Thurston, 44
  Story of Kennett, H

Taylor, B:, author of
  Theoph. Trent, H 1965
Taylor, G:, author of
  Antinous, H385
Taylor, Ja. W.,
  Victim of Intrigue, H 1810
Tecumseh, character in
  Elkswatawa, H 1885
  Eoneguski, H 1890
  Men of the Backwoods,
  Red Eagle, H 1895
  Western Captive, H
Temple,
  For the Temple, H340
Tenney, E: P., author of
  Agamenticus, H 1085
  Constance of Acadia, H
Texas, scenes of
  Ambrosio, H 2040
  Inez, H 2045
  Old Hicks, the Guide, H
  Remember, H 2045
Thackeray, W: M., author
  Adventures of Philip, 1632
  Kickleburys, 477
  Lovel the Widower, 1490
  Newcombs, The, 1617
  Pendennis, 1675
  Virginians, H 1110
Thais, H280
Theodora, character in
  Struggle for Rome,
Theodoric, character in
  Struggle for Rome,
Theoph. Trent, H 1965
Thirty Tyrants, char. in
  Charmione, H115
Thirty-nine Men for One
  Woman, H 760
Thomas, Martha M., author of
  Capt. Phil, H 2235
Thompson, Dan. P., author of
  Ethan Allen, H 1245
  Green Mt. Boys, H 1170
  May Martin, H 1730
  Rangers, H 1240
Thorny Path, H420
Thrasybulis, char. in
  Charmione, H115
Three Greek Children, 1187
Three Judges, H 845
Throne of David, H40
Through Colonial Doorways, H 1650
Tiberius, char. in
  Dion, H285

12

INDEX.

Ticonderoga, H 1055
Tiernan, M. F., author of
  Jack Horner, H 2265
Tiffany, Osmond, author
  Brandon, H 1060
Tinsley ( ), author of
  Priest of the Nile, H26
Tokeah, H 1060
Tourgee, A. W., author of
  Buttons' Inn, 206, H
  Figs and Thistles, 247
  Hot Ploughshares, H
Traitor, H 1815
Traitor,
  Roman Traitor, H170
Traits of the Tea-party,
  H 1195
Travelers, H 1980
Travels of Anacharsis,
  H125
Treasure-House,
  King's Treasure
  House, H27
Treasure Island, H 965
Tripoli, scene of
  Decatur and Somers.
Trowbridge, J: T., author
  Burr-cliff, 10s
  Coupon Bonds,18
  Cudjo's Cave, H 2200
  Farnell's Folly, 31
  Father Brighthopes, 246
  Lucy Arlyn, 300
  Martin Merryvale, 51h
  Neighbor Jackwood, 93.
  Old Battle-ground, 100
True Stories, H 675
True Womanhood, H 2170
Tucker, Beverly, author
  Partisan Leader, H 2195
Tucker, St. G;, author of
  George Balcomb, H 1700
  Hansford, H 870
Twice Taken, H 1015
Twicetold Tales, H 660
Two Hundred Years Ago,
  H 785
Two Little Confederates,
  H 2250
Two Thousand Years
  Ago, H170
Tyre,
  King of Tyre, 1185
Uarda, H30
Uncle Tom's Cabin, H
  2010
Underwood, Fr., author of
  Man's Proposes, 305
  Quabbin, H 2000
Upham, E:, author of
  Rameses, H25

Valerius, H220, 365
Van Gelder Papers, H
Vasconselos, H 600
Vermont, scene of
  Green Mt. Boys, H 1170
  May Martin, H 1730
  Neighbor Jackwood, H
Verne, J., author of
  Family Without a Name,
Verrazzano, in
  Y. F.'s Amer. Explorers,
Verri, A., author of
  Roman Nights, H205
Victim of Intrigue, H
  1810
Victoria, H 775
Victorious Defeat, H 1745
Victory of the Vanquished, H240
Virginia, scene of
  Among the Camps, H
  2275
  Brandon, H 1060
  Cavaliers, H 860
  Don Miff, H 2240
  Fairfax, H 1025
  George Stalden, H 1115
  Hammer and Rapier, H
  H: St. John, H 1215
  His Great Self, H 982
  In Ole Va., H 2145
  Journal, H 1755
  Judith, H 2025
  Justin Harley, H 1150
  Knights, H 980
  Last of the Foresters, H
  My Lady Pocahontas, H
    635
  Old Jack, H 2205
  On Newfound River, H
  Orlando, H 1130
  Puritan, H 810
  Swallow Barn, H 2005
  Two Little Confederates.
  Virginia Comedians, H
  Virginians, H 1110
  With Lee, H 2280
  Youth Jefferson, H 1105
Virginians, H 1110
Visit to Ancient Rome,
  H200
Wacousta, H 1910
Wallace, Lew, author of
  Ben Hur, H250
  Fair God, H 565
Walloth, W:, author of
  King's Treasure
  House, H27
War, 401-404, in
—, 236-220, in
  Salammbo, H145
—, 218-211, in

Young Carthagenian,
Ward, H. D., author of
  Master of the Magicians. H60
Ware, W:, author of
  Julian, H270
  Probus, H441
  Zenobia, H440
Warner, C: D., author of
  Life of Smith, H 640
Wash Bolter, H 2120
Washington, scene of
  Honest J: Vane, H 2285
  Justine's Lovers, H
  Scenes in W—, H 1840
Washington, G:, char. in
  Brandon, H 1060
  Colonial Boy, H 630
  Guert Ten Eyck, H
  Life of, H 1645
  Near to Nature's Heart,
    H 1345
  Pemberton, H 1460
  Spur of Monmouth, H
  Virginians, H 1110
  Wash. and His Generals, H 1565
  Wilderness, H 1035
  With Wolfe, H 1085
Water Witch, H 865
Watson, A (C.) author of
  Old Harbor Town, H
Watson, H. (C.), author of
  Camp Fires, H 1583
Watson, J. C., author of
  Tales of the Times, H
Waunangee, H 1925
Webb, Mrs., Martyrs of
  Carthage, 415
Webber, C: W., author of
  Old Hicks the Guide, H
Wedding, description of
  Charicles, H135
Weir, Ja., author of
  Lonz Powers, H 1715
  Simon Kenton, H 1590
Wept of Wish-ton-wish, H
  830
West-Virginia, scene of
  Young, or the Rescue, H
  Western Captive, H 1665
  Westward Ho! H 1695
Whalley, character in
  Mt. Hope, H 840
  Three Judges, H 845
Wharton, A. H., author
  Thron' Colonial, H 1650
Wheeler, J. A. T., author
  Herodotus, H95
Whisky Rebellion, in
  Modern Chivalry, H

13

White, J: Silas, editor Boys' Herodotus, H 97 Boy's Plutarch, H 143
White, J: T., author of Knight of the Golden Mellice, H 710
White Chief, H 711
White, Peregrine, char. in Peep at Pilgrims, H
Whittier, J: G., author of Leaves fr. Margaret Smith's J., H 875
Wildenbruch, E. author Master of Tanagra, 127
Wilderness, H 1035
Willett, W: M., author of Herod, H185
Williamsburg, scene of Youth of Jefferson, H
Wilmer, L. A., author of De Soto, H 605
Wilson, A. J. (E.), author Inez, H 2045
Winslow, Gov., char. in Peep at Pilgrims, H
Winthrop, Gov. J:, char. in Merry Mount, H 685

Peep at Pilgrims, H
Winthrop, Th., author of Cecil Dreeme, 208 E. Brothertoft, H 1610 John Brent, 62
Wiseman, N:, author of Fabiola, H450
Witch of New England, H 925
Witchcraft, described in Delusion, H 930 Martha Corey, H 945 Naomi, H 790 Salem Witchcraft, H South Meadows, H 940 Witch of New-England, With Lee, H 2260 With Wolfe, H 1065 Within the Capes, H 1940
Wolfe, Gen. Ja., char. in Brandon, H 1060 Haverhill, H 1070 With Wolfe, H 1065
Woman of Shawmut, H 1000
Wright, H., A., author Stories of Persons, H

Wright, H. C., author of Children's Stories, H
Wyandotte, H 1225
Wyoming, Pa., scene of Mary Derwent, H 1380
Yemassee, H 983
Yorktown, H 1505
Young, or the Rescue, H 1670
Young Carthagenian, H150
Young Folk's Amer. Explor., H 590
Young Folk's Hist. Boston, H 1210
Young Folk's Amer. Ex-War, H 2293
Young Patroon, H 915
Youth of Jefferson, H 1105
Youth of the Old Dominion, H 625
Zachary Phipps, H 1835
Zenobia, H440
Zoroaster, H65
Zury, H 1970

14

www.ingramcontent.com/pod-product-compliance
Lightning Source LLC
Chambersburg PA
CBHW020155170426
43199CB00010B/1047